Addiction

Psychological Disorders

Psychological
Disorders

Addiction

Vatsal G. Thakkar, M.D.

Series Editor
Christine Collins, Ph.D.

Foreword by
Pat Levitt, Ph.D.
Vanderbilt Kennedy
Center for Research
on Human Development

CHELSEA HOUSE
PUBLISHERS
An imprint of Infobase Publishing

Addiction

Chelsea House
An imprint of Infobase Publishing
132 West 31st Street
New York NY 10001

Library of Congress Cataloging-in-Publication Data

Thakkar, Vatsal G.
  Addiction/ Vatsal G. Thakkar.
    p. cm. — (Pyschological disorders)
  Includes bibliographical references and index.
  ISBN 0-7910-8539-2 (hardcover)
  1. Substance abuse—Juvenile literature. 2. Compulsive behavior—Juvenile literature. I. Title. II. Psychological disorders (Chelsea House Publishers)
  RC564.3T33 2006
   616.86'—dc22   2006004995

Chelsea House books are available at special discounts when purchased in bulk quantities for businesses, associations, institutions, or sales promotions. Please call our Special Sales Department in New York at (212) 967-8800 or (800) 322-8755.

You can find Chelsea House on the World Wide Web at http://www.chelseahouse.com

Text and cover design by Keith Trego

Printed in the United States of America

Bang EJB 10 9 8 7 6 5 4 3 2

This book is printed on acid-free paper.

Table of Contents

Foreword

Pat Levitt, Ph.D.
Vanderbilt Kennedy
Center for Research
on Human Development

Think of the most complicated aspect of our universe, and then multiply that by infinity! Even the most enthusiastic of mathematicians and physicists acknowledge that the brain is by far the most challenging entity to understand. By design, the human brain is made up of billions of cells called neurons, which use chemical neurotransmitters to communicate with each other through connections called synapses. Each brain cell has about 2,000 synapses. Connections between neurons are not formed in a random fashion, but rather, are organized into a type of architecture that is far more complex than any of today's supercomputers. And, not only is the brain's connective architecture more complex than any computer, its connections are capable of *changing* to improve the way a circuit functions. For example, the way we learn new information involves changes in circuits that actually improve performance. Yet some change can also result in a disruption of connections, like changes that occur in disorders such as drug addiction, depression, schizophrenia, and epilepsy, or even changes that can increase a person's risk of suicide.

Genes and the environment are powerful forces in building the brain during development and ensuring normal brain functioning, but they can also be the root causes of psychological and neurological disorders when things go awry. The way in which brain architecture is built before birth and in childhood will determine how well the brain functions when we are adults, and even how susceptible we are to such diseases as depression, anxiety, or attention disorders, which can severely disturb brain function. In a sense, then, understanding how the brain is built can lead us to a clearer picture of the ways in which our brain works, how we can improve its functioning, and what we can do to repair it when diseases strike.

Brain architecture reflects the highly specialized jobs that are performed by human beings, such as seeing, hearing, feeling, smelling, and moving. Different brain areas are specialized to control specific functions. Each specialized area must communicate well with other areas for the brain to accomplish even more complex tasks, like controlling body physiology—our patterns of sleep, for example, or even our eating habits, both of which can become disrupted if brain development or function is disturbed in some way. The brain controls our feelings, fears, and emotions; our ability to learn and store new information; and how well we recall old information. The brain does all this, and more, by building, during development, the circuits that control these functions, much like a hard-wired computer. Even small abnormalities that occur during early brain development through gene mutations, viral infection, or fetal exposure to alcohol can increase the risk of developing a wide range of psychological disorders later in life.

Those who study the relationship between brain architecture and function, and the diseases that affect this bond, are neuroscientists. Those who study and treat the disorders that are caused by changes in brain architecture and chemistry are psychiatrists and psychologists. Over the last 50 years, we have learned quite a lot about how brain architecture and chemistry work and how genetics contribute to brain structure and function. Genes are very important in controlling the initial phases of building the brain. In fact, almost every gene in the human genome is needed to build the brain. This process of brain development actually starts prior to birth, with almost all the neurons we will ever have in our brain produced by mid-gestation. The assembly of the architecture, in the form of intricate circuits, begins by this time, and by birth, we have the basic organization laid out. But the work is not yet complete, because billions of connections form over a remarkably long period of time, extending through puberty. The brain of a child is being built and modified on a daily basis, even during sleep.

While there are thousands of chemical building blocks, such as proteins, lipids, and carbohydrates, that are used, much like bricks and mortar, to put the architecture together, the highly detailed connectivity that emerges during childhood depends greatly upon experiences and our environment. In building a house, we use specific blueprints to assemble the basic structures, like a foundation, walls, floors, and ceilings. The brain is assembled similarly. Plumbing and electricity, like the basic circuitry of the brain, are put in place early in the building process. But for all of this early work, there is another very important phase of development, which is termed experience-dependent development. During the first three years of life, our brains actually form far more connections than we will ever need, almost 40% more! Why would this occur? Well, in fact, the early circuits form in this way so that we can use experience to mold our brain architecture to best suit the functions that we are likely to need for the rest of our lives.

Experience is not just important for the circuits that control our senses. A young child who experiences toxic stress, like physical abuse, will have his or her brain architecture changed in regions that will result in poorer control of emotions and feelings as an adult. Experience is powerful. When we repeatedly practice on the piano or shoot a basketball hundreds of times daily, we are using experience to model our brain connections to function at their finest. Some will achieve better results than others, perhaps because the initial phases of circuit-building provided a better base, just like the architecture of houses may differ in terms of their functionality. We are working to understand the brain structure and function that result from the powerful combination of genes building the initial architecture and a child's experience adding the all-important detailed touches. We also know that, like an old home, the architecture can break down. The aging process can be particularly hard on the ability of brain circuits to function at their best because positive change comes less readily as we get older. Synapses may be lost and brain chemistry can change over time. The difficulties in understanding how architecture gets built are paralleled by the complexities of what happens to that architecture as we grow older. Dementia associated with brain deterioration as a complication of Alzheimer's disease, or memory loss associated with aging or alcoholism are active avenues of research in the neuroscience community.

There is truth, both for development and in aging, in the old adage "use it or lose it." Neuroscientists are pursuing the idea that brain architecture and chemistry can be modified well beyond childhood. If we understand the mechanisms that make it easy for a young, healthy brain to learn or repair itself following an accident, perhaps we can use those same tools to optimize the functioning of aging brains. We already know many ways in which we can improve the functioning of the aging or injured brain. For example, for an individual who has suffered a stroke that has caused structural damage to brain architecture, physical exercise can be quite powerful in helping to reorganize circuits so that they function better, even in an elderly individual. And you know that when you exercise and sleep regularly, you just feel better. Your brain chemistry and architecture are functioning at their best. Another example of ways we can improve nervous system function are the drugs that are used to treat mental illnesses. These drugs are designed to change brain chemistry so that the neurotransmitters used for communication between brain cells can function more normally. These same types of drugs, however, when taken in excess or abused, can actually damage brain chemistry and change brain architecture so that it functions more poorly.

As you read the series Psychological Disorders, the images of altered brain organization and chemistry will come to mind in thinking about complex diseases such as schizophrenia or drug addiction. There is nothing more fascinating and important to understand for the well-being of humans. But also keep in mind that as neuroscientists, we are on a mission to comprehend human nature, the way we perceive the world, how we recognize color, why we smile when thinking about the Thanksgiving turkey, the emotion of experiencing our first kiss, or how we can remember the winner of the 1953 World Series. If you are interested in people, and the world in which we live, you are a neuroscientist, too.

Pat Levitt, Ph.D.
Director, Vanderbilt Kennedy Center
for Research on Human Development
Vanderbilt University
Nashville, Tennessee

Introduction 1

LAURA'S STORY

Nineteen-year-old Laura was given speed (methamphetamine tablets) back in high school by a friend when she complained that she didn't have enough time to do all her schoolwork. She found that when she used it, she experienced a surge of energy and was able to stay up late, focus, and do well on her exams. Now Laura is a college student at a private liberal arts school, where she has continued her occasional use of speed. During final exams her freshman year, Laura used speed on a daily basis. That summer, she noticed for the first time that she felt the need to use speed outside of school. Without it, she felt tired and depressed. When she took it, she felt energetic and vivacious. She spent most of the money she earned at her summer job on speed, using the drug several times a week.

Now back in college as a sophomore, Laura is using speed almost every day. She even skips classes sometimes, either because she is on speed and feels too wired to sit still or because she is crashing from the drug's effects and is too tired to make it through a one-hour lecture. She finds that the amount of the drug that used to help her focus and study doesn't have the same effect anymore, so she has doubled and even tripled her intake. Going more than a day or two without speed makes her so irritable that her roommate has threatened to move out. Laura has failed three out of five of her midterms and even her parents, who live several hours away, have noticed a change in Laura's behavior. Her boyfriend, who has tried speed but didn't like it, calls her a "junkie" and breaks up with her. This sends Laura into a tailspin. She spends a solid week in her dorm room, crying much of the time and telling her roommate that she may kill herself. The roommate calls the campus counseling center and is advised to bring Laura in for an evaluation.

How did the life of this casual user of an illegal drug get so out of control? This is the story of **addiction**. Addiction is a

Degrees of Drug Use

1. **Experimental Use**—This is usually the type of "first use" that occurs due to curiosity or the encouragement of friends or family members.

2. **Recreational Use**—This is the next stage of drug use that occurs when the mind-altering properties are enjoyed and there don't seem to be any negative consequences. Recreational use usually occurs in groups as a shared experience.

3. **Circumstantial Use**—This develops when the drug is used for a specific effect or to deal with a specific problem. It may be used in groups, with strangers, or alone. Drug use may fluctuate over time and occur in binges.

4. **Compulsive Use**—This is drug addiction. The user's life is dominated by getting and using the drug. Everything else is less important. Addicts may be able to function quite well as long as they have access to the drug and use it in a regulated way, but their use can easily become uncontrollable and lead to physical, social, and legal problems.

Source: Gahlinger, Paul M. "Drug Use and Abuse." *Illegal Drugs: A Complete Guide to Their History, Chemistry, Use, and Abuse*. Las Vegas: Sagebrush Press, 2001, p. 90.

disease that often operates in stealth, making the user believe there is no problem and that his or her actions are totally under control.

ADDICTION

What is drug abuse? What is addiction? Many people drink alcohol, smoke cigarettes, and drink coffee. Is this abuse or addiction? Through the years, society has determined which drugs should be freely permitted (such as caffeine), which drugs should be controlled or regulated (such as nicotine and alcohol), which drugs should be used only for medical purposes (cocaine and morphine), and which should be completely banned (methamphetamine, LSD, and many others). These categories were set up as scientists learned that the use of certain substances caused more harm than good. In the United States today, you have to be at least 18 years old to buy tobacco products. You must be 21 years old to buy alcohol. There is a list several pages long of drugs you cannot legally buy, no matter how old you are.

Addiction has affected many millions of people in the United States. Some of those affected are the spouses of addicts. Some are children or other family members. Others are victims of crimes such as theft, violence, or drunk driving—crimes that are fueled by addiction. As a society, we all are touched by addiction through government expenditures on health care and the legal system. The two biggest addictions in the United States—cigarettes and alcohol—cost the health-care system over $100 billion per year. The United States has more drug offenders behind bars than any other industrialized country in the world. Drug use and addiction is an important subject for study, not only for those interested in human health, but for all citizens, so that we can better understand what addiction is and why it happens.

Figure 1.1 Cigarettes and alcohol are the two most widely used addictive substances in the United States today.

WHAT IS ADDICTION?

Addiction is a very difficult word to define. Different people sometimes have drastically different definitions. For our purposes, we will define addiction as a medical and **psychiatric** condition characterized by the compulsive overuse of a substance that continues in the face of negative and even catastrophic consequences to the user's life.

These negative consequences may include the loss of good relationships with friends and family members. They may include loss of a job and of one's life savings. The drug user may even continue to use when he or she knows that the drug use will eventually kill him or her. This can be seen in **emphysema** patients who continue to smoke cigarettes while connected to oxygen tanks, or cocaine addicts who keep using even after suffering heart attacks. Addiction is a very powerful phenomenon.

Substance dependence is another term for addiction. In the medical community, it is the preferred term because the word *addiction* has so many negative connotations. We can divide addiction, or dependence, into two types: physical and psychological. **Physical dependence** is when a person grows biologically accustomed to a substance through regular exposure. **Psychological dependence** is the craving or preoccupation surrounding the use of a certain substance. In Laura's case, described earlier, the addiction started with a psychological dependence, but ultimately became a strong physical dependence as well. Addiction typically includes facets of both physical and psychological dependence.

Our bodies go through certain changes when we take in foreign substances. We feel the immediate effects of a drug, but over time, our bodies counteract these effects. This happens not only with alcohol, tobacco, and illicit drugs, but also with prescription treatments such as blood pressure and diabetes medications. This process is called **tolerance**. Here's an example. Let's say someone tries coffee for the first time. He may have trouble sleeping because he is not "used to" caffeine—the biologically active drug in the coffee. But if he begins to drink coffee every day, the effects diminish, as the body gets used to the daily caffeine. Over time, the body becomes physically dependent on caffeine.

Another feature that illustrates this dependence is **withdrawal**. This happens when a substance that the body has become accustomed to is taken away. If a daily coffee drinker suddenly stops drinking coffee, he or she may experience symptoms such as headache, fatigue, and irritability. After a few days without coffee, however, the body will readjust to being caffeine-free.

DIAGNOSING ADDICTION

The clinical specialties that treat patients with addiction are typically psychology and psychiatry The major psychiatric reference book, the *Diagnostic and Statistical Manual of Mental*

Movies About Addiction

- *Rush* (Jason Patric and Jennifer Jason Leigh)—A story of two undercover narcotics agents
- *Traffic* (Michael Douglas, Catherine Zeta-Jones, Benicio del Toro)—Interwoven stories of drug use culminating with the daughter of the United States drug czar
- *New Jack City* (Ice-T, Wesley Snipes, Chris Rock)—An urban tale of a cop taking on a drug kingpin; shows a horrifying portrayal of drug withdrawal
- *Blow* (Johnny Depp, Penelope Cruz)—Based on the true rags-to-riches-to-incarceration story of real-life cocaine supplier George Jung
- *When a Man Loves a Woman* (Andy Garcia, Meg Ryan)—A story about a female alcoholic and the impact of her addiction on her family
- *28 Days* (Sandra Bullock)—A newspaper reporter spends 28 days in an drug and alcohol rehabilitation facility
- *Leaving Las Vegas* (Nicholas Cage, Elizabeth Shue)—An alcoholic loses his job and moves to Las Vegas to go on a last drinking binge

Disorders, Fourth Edition (DSM-IV), uses the term *substance dependence* for addiction and defines it as a pattern of substance use that leads to clinically significant impairment or distress. This means that the substance use interferes with some aspect of life—whether it is school, work, or relationships with loved ones. For a condition to qualify as substance dependence, three or more of the following signs or symptoms must be present: tolerance, withdrawal, a need for **intoxication,**

Did You Know?

- Alcohol is the most widely used mind-altering drug in the United States.
- Marijuana is the most commonly used illegal drug in the United States.
- Alcohol is actually given as a medical treatment in cases of methanol or ethylene glycol poisoning.
- There is enough nicotine in a cigarette to kill a child. Only a small portion of this nicotine is released into the body by smoking.
- The phrase *cold turkey* comes from the description of a person's skin during opiate (narcotic) withdrawal—the skin gets bumpy, cold, and clammy.
- Sigmund Freud, the influential Austrian psychiatrist, was addicted to tobacco and cocaine for most of his life; in fact, he died from cancer of the mouth.
- The Beatles song "Lucy in the Sky with Diamonds" is believed to be about the hallucinations caused by LSD.
- William Shakespeare may have used marijuana. Analysis of pipe fragments from his home showed traces of cannabis.

escalating degrees of use or great amounts of time spent acquiring the substance, an inability to stop using, or continued use even in the face of harm to health (such as an ulcer caused by drinking alcohol).

For a mental health professional to diagnose substance dependence, or addiction, the patient must have not only the physical and psychological symptoms, but also the personal dysfunction that goes along with them. This makes the definition of addiction vary from one person to the next. Whereas some people may be able to consume 10 alcoholic drinks in a day without it having an immediate effect on their lives, others may experience personal ruin by drinking 6 alcoholic drinks a day, qualifying for a diagnosis of alcohol dependence.

REASONS FOR DRUG USE

People use drugs for a variety of reasons. Some are bored or curious and want to adventure into an altered mental state. Some experience very stressful life events that make them to want to escape. Some use drugs because their friends do so and they feel pressured into going along. Some enjoy the intoxication and want to seek out this pleasure as often as possible. Some have very serious psychiatric problems such as anxiety or depression, and are looking for relief from their symptoms. Others have a severe mental disorder such as the hallucinations of schizophrenia and are looking to ease these symptoms.

For whatever reason different people use drugs and alcohol, the result is usually the same: The body gets used to the substance and the person eventually becomes addicted.

A Brief History of Addiction

All substances are poisons; there is none which is not a poison.
The right dose differentiates a poison and a remedy.
—Famous Swiss physician Paracelsus (1493–1541)

In wise hands, poison is medicine.
In foolish hands, medicine is a poison.
—Venetian adventurer Giacomo Casanova (1725–1798)

OPIUM

Opium was the first recorded substance to be used for its medicinal and tranquilizing effects. Opium is a milky white fluid that comes from the bulb of an opium poppy. The first evidence of its use dates back to Mesopotamia in 4,000 B.C. Over the millennia, it has taken various forms that have allowed it to be chewed, burned, inhaled, or mixed with fermented liquids. The ancient Greek poet Homer wrote in *The Odyssey* about an opium mixture that helped "lull all pain and bring forth forgetfulness." Today, chemical cousins of opium, such as morphine, are used as **analgesics** (pain relievers).

Opium's dark side, its addictive potential, was mentioned in Egyptian medical texts thousands of years ago. Nevertheless, it was widely used until the mid-nineteenth century. People attributed the same characteristics to opiate addiction as they

Figure 2.1 Opium is extracted as a milky substance from the bulb of the opium poppy plant.

did to tobacco addiction—it was a bad habit and a nuisance but it was believed to be relatively safe. Opium addiction gained notoriety in 1821 with the publication of *Confessions of an English Opium Eater* by English essayist Thomas de Quincey. De Quincey discovered opium as a 17-year-old college student and struggled with addiction for the rest of his life. He described it as "Divine poppy-juice, as indispensable as breathing," and noted that he experienced severe withdrawal symptoms when he tried to quit—nightmares, **paranoia**, and the feeling of being buried alive. Many addiction specialists say that opiate withdrawal is probably the most disturbing and uncomfortable experience known to humankind, outside of bodily injury.

ALCOHOL

Although opium was likely the world's first mood-altering substance, alcohol seems to have been nature's first addictive one. This is because the potency of opium in its original form was fairly low—its addictive potential wasn't revealed until much later. Alcohol, on the other hand, could be prepared in large batches and consumed in great quantities. Like most drugs, alcohol was originally considered divine—a gift from the ancestors of prehistoric humans. There has been evidence of alcohol use in ceremonies and festivals dating back 8,000 years. The discovery of the process of alcohol production is hard to trace, since it can be made virtually spontaneously with the right ingredients.

A Persian story tells of a king named Jamshid who stored grape juice in large jars. Jamshid accidentally left one jar open to the air, and over time, the juice fermented and turned into wine. Jamshid thought the juice was ruined and had it labeled as poison. One of his concubines, intending to commit suicide, drank the fermented "poison" and was surprised to find that instead of killing her, it cured her headache. Thus, a new intoxicating beverage was born and the king began to make more of it.

One of the first historical references to addiction can be found on the tomb of an Egyptian king who lived more than 5,000 years ago. The inscription on the tomb reads: "His earthly abode was rent and shattered by wine and beer. And the spirit escaped before it was called for." It seems clear by this translation that the king suffered from alcoholism, which led to his early death.

Of course, once the addictive effects of alcohol became widely known, it was inevitable that society would want to place limits on its use. The earliest record of this occurred around 4,000 years ago, when the Babylonian king Hammurabi restricted the consumption and sale of alcohol. The punishment for violating

Figure 2.2 People have been drinking beer since ancient times, as seen in this painting created in Egypt around 1350 B.C., which shows a Syrian soldier drinking beer with his wife and child.

these laws was death. China also enacted laws to control alcohol use. The government executed people who were drunk in public. In almost every society throughout history, there has been some type of restriction placed on the production, sale, or use of alcohol. In twenty-first century America, there are restrictions on all three.

NEW WAYS TO TAKE DRUGS

There was a long span of time between discovering the potential of alcohol addiction and noticing the addictive qualities of other substances. This is because, until the eighteenth century, there was no efficient method of using or abusing other **psychoactive** substances. Then, two American inventions came along. The first was the smoking pipe. Although the pipe was probably invented 2,000 years ago by Native Americans, it did not reach widespread popularity as a means for drug **ingestion** until the seventeenth and eighteenth centuries in most of the world.

A smoking pipe (including a cigarette, which can be considered a single-use pipe) is a very efficient and potent method of ingesting a drug. Burning a substance releases the raw chemical molecules, which get inhaled then move from the lungs into the bloodstream within seconds. From the blood, they are on a direct path to the brain.

Burning also has another effect, which is to create new intoxicating chemicals by combustion—something that does not occur with any other method of drug ingestion. Not only is there a larger amount of the target drug, but there are also large amounts of various psychoactive drugs ingested, all of them going directly to the brain. Compare this process to swallowing a drug. The drug goes to the stomach, is dissolved by acids and enzymes, then gets absorbed through the small intestine into the bloodstream. It does not go directly to the brain, however, since the liver, the body's filtering organ, works to metabolize the drug before it makes its way to the brain. This is why the most widely used and most addictive drugs today are those that can be smoked. Tobacco, cocaine, heroin, and marijuana all fall into this category.

The hypodermic syringe was the second American invention that propelled the occurrence of addiction to the level at which

The Four Categories of Psychoactive Substances:

1. No medical value, no abuse potential
   a) Examples are certain herbal remedies and homeopathic treatments.
   b) These are generally considered to be safe for use by adults.

2. Medical value, no abuse potential
   a) These are medications available either over the counter or by prescription; these include the vast majority of herbal and medicinal remedies.
   b) Examples include aspirin (derived from tree bark) and digitalis (heart medication derived from a plant). Neither of these has been shown to have addictive qualities.

3. Medical value and abuse potential
   a) These drugs are available by prescription and are controlled by government laws, namely the Controlled Substances Act (Schedules II–V).
   b) Examples include morphine (an opiate pain medication) and Ritalin® (methylphenidate) used in the treatment of narcolepsy and attention-deficit/hyperactivity disorder (ADHD).

4. No medical value, but having abuse potential
   a) These drugs are found in Schedule I of the Controlled Substances Act.
   b) All of these substances are illegal for possession or medical use.
   c) Examples include heroin and LSD.

it exists today. Injecting involves crushing a drug, mixing it with fluid, and shooting it directly into a vein, usually in the arm. Although this method is almost as efficient as burning and inhaling a substance, the only reason it is less popular is because it is more invasive—it requires the piercing of skin and pain, making it unpleasant to many people. In addition, injecting drugs carries the risk of infection with diseases like HIV and hepatitis. Burning and inhaling a drug is much more common, as evidenced by the widespread use of cigarettes in today's society.

The reason these two inventions sparked more addiction is because the efficient delivery more rapidly exposed the brain to the mind-altering drug, creating a "**rush**." The use of smoking and injection quickly spread, and the world quickly saw the rise of drug addiction. It was not long afterward that countries and governments began to place limits on the availability and use of certain substances. In China, for example, the government banned the importation and use of opium in the 1830s. In the United States, all substances were legal until the early twentieth century, when the government began to place controls on narcotics (opiates), alcohol, marijuana, and finally, on all serious mind-altering substances.

The Controlled Substances Act (CSA) of 1970 was the first attempt by the U.S. government to consolidate the different laws on drugs into one general code. The CSA classifies drugs into four types: opiates and opioids, hallucinogens, stimulants, and depressants. It also groups the drugs into five categories, called schedules. Schedule I includes the most addictive drugs, which have no medicinal benefit. The drugs on Schedules II–V have medical benefits and may be used under the proper authority—drugs in Schedule V are considered to be the least addictive.

THE WAR AGAINST DRUGS

This brings us to the present day and age. The strict prohibitions on drug possession by government and law enforcement officials, along with a "Just Say No" mindset, has led to the idea that any level of drug use leads to criminal behavior and addiction. Although this is not true, the rigid drug laws in effect in the United States suggest otherwise. For example, in New York State, a first-time nonviolent offense for possessing 4 ounces (113 grams) of cocaine can carry a minimum sentence of 15 years, the same as the sentence for murder.[1]

Society has determined that drugs and other substances of abuse are dangerous both to the users and to others. In free countries, we believe the individual should be allowed to determine his or her own fate, except when it may cause excessive harm. For example, alcohol is legal for adults, but there are laws to prevent people from driving a vehicle while intoxicated, to promote public safety. People are allowed to smoke tobacco products but are often prevented from doing so inside certain buildings to protect the health of others.

Besides the danger of harming other people, another principle used in determining whether a drug or substance should be legal is the nature of its mind-altering effects. All the drugs that are banned by the U.S. government produce physical and psychological effects that can be severe and unpredictable. Therefore, these substances are restricted from personal use, except in rare cases under the supervision of a medical professional. Certain drugs may sometimes be legally prescribed by a physician but inappropriately used by the patient to achieve a certain effect. This is called an **illicit** use of a legitimate drug.

As a general rule, drugs that are legal (such as caffeine, nicotine, and alcohol), cause more physical effects than psychological effects, although they can cause both. Drugs that are illegal (like LSD, cocaine, and heroin) cause more psychological effects than physical effects, although they, too, can cause both. The latter category of drugs can cause severe psychological distress, leading users to hallucinate, become violent, or withdraw into their own worlds, even to the point of self-starvation or suicide. Because an addicted person will continue to take the drug even in the face of these dangers, drug abuse is a serious problem for society.

3 Causes of Addiction

RATES OF ALCOHOL AND DRUG USE AND ADDICTION

The vast majority of Americans use some drug that is designed to have an effect on the mind. If you include all available mind-altering substances (caffeine, nicotine, alcohol, and illicit and prescription drugs), the percentage of American users reaches 95%.[2] At least half of the U.S. population engages in alcohol use. Heavy use, bordering on alcoholism, is estimated to affect some 7% of the population, mostly men. Nicotine products are used by 30% of the population, but the rate of use is about 40% among the 18–25 age group. Marijuana is the most common illicit drug used by Americans, although its use has been decreasing since 1979. Approximately 6% of Americans use marijuana at least once a month. Cocaine use reached its peak in the 1980s and has been declining ever since. Currently, cocaine is used by approximately 1% of the U.S. population. Around 2 million Americans have tried heroin, and 120,000 are current users.[3] Why do so many people use drugs and alcohol? Why do millions suffer from addiction?

DRUGS AND THE BRAIN

It is difficult to learn about addiction without understanding the organ in which addiction takes place—the human brain. The brain is our most complex and least understood organ. Everything that we do, think, feel, or dream happens in the

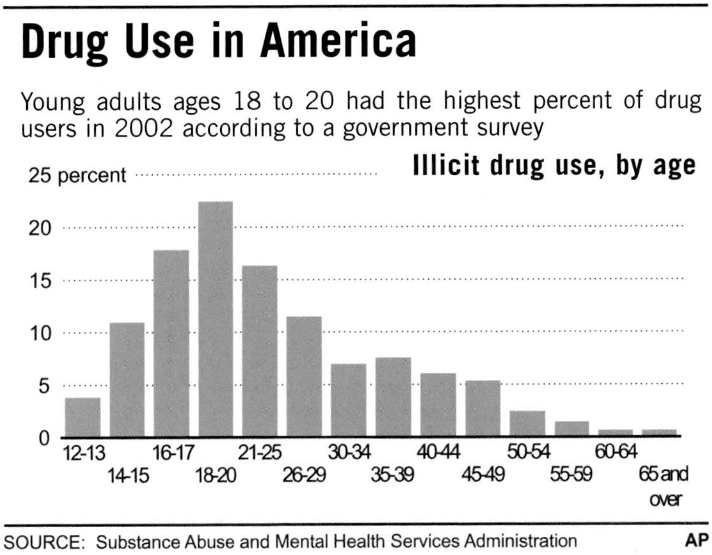
Drug Use in America
Young adults ages 18 to 20 had the highest percent of drug users in 2002 according to a government survey
Illicit drug use, by age
25 percent
20
15
10
5
0
12-13
14-15
16-17
18-20
21-25
26-29
30-34
35-39
40-44
45-49
50-54
55-59
60-64
65 and over
SOURCE: Substance Abuse and Mental Health Services Administration
AP

Figure 3.1 Young people between the ages of 18 and 20 make up the highest percentage of drug users, according to this 2002 study.

brain. Anything we experience through any of our five senses also happens in the brain. When we touch the point of a needle, receptors on our skin send a signal through nerves in the hand and arm, into the spinal cord, and finally to the brain. The brain assesses this signal and reacts to it, perhaps by moving the finger away from the sharp point. The same thing happens when we smell a rose. Receptors in our nose react to the molecules in the air and associate that combination of molecules with a rose, an interpretation that is made in the brain. Even basic bodily functions such as breathing, heartbeat, and the passage of urine and excrement are regulated by the brain.

The brain weighs about 3 pounds (1.4 kg) and is made up of individual nerve cells, called **neurons.** The average brain consists of 100 billion neurons. They have an oblong shape and have several parts. You can imagine the brain as one big tangle of neurons. Neurons extend from one area to another, and sometimes the same neuron extends to multiple areas. The brain's 100 billion neurons then make 1,000 trillion connections by the time the human brain is fully developed.

Neurotransmitters are protein substances that nerve cells produce to communicate with each other. Different neurotransmitters are active in different parts of the brain and have different functions. All drugs that are used to alter perceptions, states of consciousness, or moods act on the brain. These include things such as caffeine, prescription medications, and illicit drugs like cocaine and heroin. The actions of these drugs occur at the molecular level.

A biologically active drug exerts its influence over some bodily organ, function, or process. All of the organs and tissues

Types of Neurotransmitters (NT):

E=excitatory; I=Inhibitory

Norepinephrine—E; provides the "zest for life"; it is responsible for energy, drive, motivation, and creativity

Serotonin—E; involved in mood and anxiety regulation, as well as body temperature, sleep, appetite, and sexual function

Dopamine—E and I; involved in mood regulation and experiencing pleasure

Other neurotransmitters in the human brain include acetylcholine, glutamate, glycine, and GABA (gamma-aminobutyric acid).

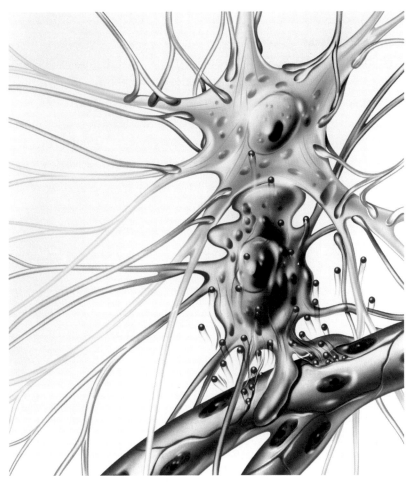

Figure 3.2 Drugs cause their effects when they get to the brain through the bloodstream. This is an artist's depiction of a drug moving from a capillary into a nerve cell of the brain.

of the body have a variety of receptors associated with them. You can think of receptors as locks that are waiting for the right key to be inserted. Once the specific drug molecule (the key) binds to a receptor (the lock), certain events occur within a cell. Almost all biological activities can be manipulated this way. Drugs can act to bind to receptors (sometimes blocking other molecules that would normally bind to them) and can either activate, deactivate, or somehow change the function of the receptor and the organ or tissue in which it is located.

Once the drug molecules are in the bloodstream, they rapidly spread throughout the body. Prescription medications, as well as illicit drugs, act on the whole body, although they are usually taken because of just one or two of their effects. Illicit drugs are most often used for their specific actions on the brain. Drugs modulate the function of various receptors, creating their desired effects as well as side effects. The net effect of the drug is to change the activity of brain cells (neurons)—making them

Methods of Drug Ingestion

- Oral ingestion (swallowing): The drug is absorbed into the bloodstream through the gastrointestinal (GI) tract.

  Examples include prescription medication tablets or alcohol.

- Inhalation: The drug is absorbed into the blood through the lungs.

  Examples include albuterol inhalers (for people with asthma) or nicotine through cigarette smoke.

- Intravenous (IV) injection: The drug is introduced directly into the bloodstream, or into muscle or fat tissue, then absorbed into the blood.

  Examples include insulin shots or heroin.

- Topical administration: The drug is absorbed from the skin into the bloodstream.

  Some blood pressure and pain medications are given this way.

fire more strongly, more weakly, more often, or less often—in a certain part of the brain. This change in the activity of neurons is what causes the desired effect from a certain drug.

The human body does not like to be manipulated. Any foreign drug introduced into the body will activate biological mechanisms that try to counteract the effect of the drug. One of the ways the brain does this is to **up-regulate** or **down-regulate** receptors. Let's say a neuron has 50 receptors on its surface for molecule X, and that molecule X is hard to come by. All 50 of those receptors are just sitting and waiting for molecule X to come along. Now imagine that, suddenly, there is a lot more of molecule X than usual around the neuron, and it stays there. The neuron responds by down-regulating the receptors for molecule X, because it doesn't need 50 of them anymore. The number of receptors drops down to 10. The opposite can also happen. If the amount of molecule X drops again, the receptors can up-regulate, going back to 50 or more, because molecule X is so scarce. This receptor regulation contributes to the phenomenon of drug **tolerance**, although other mechanisms are also at work.[4]

As an example, let's look at alcohol tolerance. The first time a person drinks alcohol, he or she may be intensely affected by just half a drink. If alcohol consumption becomes a routine event, however, the effect of alcohol usually diminishes and larger amounts are needed to provide the same effect. This is drug tolerance in action.

THE ADDICTION CIRCUIT

Psychological dependence has several features. One of the main ones is that it involves the reward or pleasure center of the brain—the **nucleus accumbens (NA)**. The nucleus accumbens is a relatively tiny area that can exert its influence over the entire brain.

Neurons from nearby areas influence the NA by releasing the neurotransmitter dopamine onto the NA neurons. The brain senses this as pleasure. There are other areas of the brain involved in the "pleasure circuit," but the nucleus accumbens and the input of dopamine from nearby neurons are key components of reward and pleasure in the brain. Any time a person does something pleasurable, dopamine is released onto neurons in the nucleus accumbens, giving the person the sensation of pleasure. Just the thought of food, sex, or a certain drug can cause some release of dopamine in the nucleus accumbens, giving rise to pleasure.

This brain pathway that is involved in the sensation of pleasure is sometimes called the **addiction circuit**. It is also involved in the overuse of some chemical substances. Animal studies have shown that the repeated use of drugs is based on the activation of this circuit.[5] Often, in the brains of addicts, the addiction circuit overrides the normal functions of feeding and reproduction. In a laboratory example, a rat is exposed to cocaine and allowed to self-administer the drug. The rat will continue to take the cocaine at every opportunity, to the detriment of all other activities.[6] This is why addicts of drugs like heroin, cocaine, nicotine, and alcohol continue to use the drug in the face of life-threatening consequences, neglecting many other normal and necessary activities.

The addiction circuit only tells half the story of addiction, however. In the later stages of drug addiction, there's another reason why people continue to use drugs—to prevent **withdrawal**. As described earlier, once a person becomes "hooked," the body may go through significant withdrawal symptoms if it doesn't get the drug. These are often very unpleasant and sometimes lethal. One sure way to relieve withdrawal symptoms is to use more of the drug. This has been shown in animal studies.[7] Herein lies the vicious cycle of addiction: A person may try a drug out of curiosity, then continue to use it because of the pleasure-reward addiction circuit. Then the person cannot stop using the drug because withdrawal symptoms occur if he or she tries to stop. Before the person knows it, life is out of control.

But this is not the end of the addiction story. Let us suppose that a nicotine addict has finally, after a dozen tries, given up cigarettes. There is a significant behavioral aspect to addiction. The nicotine addict will crave a cigarette after meals because he used to smoke after every meal. He will also have to fight the urge to turn into the parking lot of his favorite convenience store, since that's what he did after work each day to buy cigarettes. Finally, for a while, he will have to avoid being with friends who still smoke or going to his favorite restaurant, where he used to light up after a meal. Inevitably, at some point in his life, no matter how hard he tries, there will come a thought, experience, memory, or feeling that triggers the craving for the drug that has been encoded in the addiction circuit.[8] This is why it is so hard for people who suffer from addiction to recover fully.

RISK FACTORS FOR ADDICTION

We know that not everybody who uses a substance or drug will get addicted to it. So how do we know who *will* be affected? The scary answer is that we can never be sure. There are certain factors, however, that can help determine who is most at risk.

One major risk factor is family history. If someone in your family has had trouble with addiction, you are at a higher risk to develop it yourself, compared with a person who has no family history of addiction. The same is true for many medical diseases like heart disease and cancer, which makes a compelling argument that addiction is related to genetic background.

Identical (**monozygotic**) twins share the same DNA (deoxyribonucleic acid; the genetic material), whereas fraternal (**dizygotic**) twins usually only share half of their genes with their twin. This helps us study the genetic transmission of a disease, since we would be more likely to see disease **concordance** (cases where both twins have the same disease) in identical twins than in fraternal twins. Studies have consistently shown that an addiction such as alcoholism has a much higher concordance among identical twins than fraternal ones, meaning it is clearly influenced by genetics.[9]

Adoptions provide another tool for the study of genetic transmission. It helps us study the **incidence** of a particular disease and decipher the influence of genetics versus the environment. For example, if a disease is purely environmental, then a child "learns" to exhibit the disease characteristic by modeling the behavior of an adult. However, we find that the biological son of an alcoholic, even if raised by nonalcoholic parents, has a much higher risk of becoming an alcoholic.[10] This makes a strong case for genetic determinants in the development of alcoholism.

Finally, another piece of genetic proof is seen in extended families. An individual is more likely to be an alcoholic if he or she has a blood relative who is an alcoholic, compared with the general population.[11] We have used alcoholism as an example because, due to the widespread use of alcohol, it has been studied most often. This shows that there are at least some genetic factors that influence who will be more likely to suffer from an addiction.

Yet another factor is exposure to drugs. Early experimentation with cigarettes and alcohol puts adolescents at a higher risk of accelerated levels (amount and type) of substance use.[12] Peer pressure and use by family members also plays a role in early experimentation.

Other factors involved in a higher risk for addiction are more debatable. There seems to be a higher risk of developing addiction among people with risk-taking personalities. Adults who were abused as children seem to make up a large percentage of the addicted population (especially addiction to alcohol), as high as 50–60%. This may be because early-life abuse may cause permanent changes in the brain, as some studies have shown, or because the person may later develop an anxiety disorder or depression that seems to be eased by alcohol or drug use.

This leads us to another factor in alcohol and drug use and addiction: Impulsivity is a personality characteristic (or, sometimes, a psychiatric symptom) that can increase a person's likelihood of using drugs. In fact, there are many psychiatric symptoms which can bring about a higher likelihood of drug or alcohol use. These can include severe depression, panic disorder, **hallucinations**, unshakeable insomnia, dread, or worry. Often, people who experience these symptoms will take alcohol or drugs either as a temporary escape, to provide relief from their symptoms and feel "normal," or as a permanent solution—that is, a daily antidote. The latter usage pattern can put people at an increased risk of addiction, especially when they do not have their psychiatric needs addressed.

In the next chapter, we look at one specific drug—nicotine—to see how people become addicted and what can be done to treat nicotine addiction.

4 Nicotine

Approximately 70 million Americans use nicotine regularly. But where does it come from? Nicotine comes from tobacco, a plant that dates back many centuries and began to be used, like most drugs, as a medicine. It was prescribed for fatigue, headaches, and infections. The most common early method of tobacco use was chewing. This continued for many years, until the nineteenth century, when French scientists isolated nicotine from tobacco as the active ingredient. Soon afterward, with the advent of the cigar and cigarette in the early 1900s, the medical community began to voice concern about the potential health risks of nicotine. Regardless, due to the new drug delivery system (inhalation), smoking took off in the United States, reaching a peak in 1960, when most men and women smoked, at least recreationally. It was around this time that medical research began to show serious health consequences from smoking.

It seems that smoking begins most often among adolescents and young adults, with the highest rate (around 40%) among 20-year-olds. From this point, it drops, although a significant portion of those who begin to smoke during adolescence will remain addicted to nicotine for the rest of their lives. Part of the reason for the high rate of addiction may be that tobacco is legal (though age-restricted), and it is hard for young people who have just started to smoke to comprehend the negative effects to their health, since the symptoms may not become apparent for

Figure 4.1 Tobacco has long been a major cash crop, especially in the southern United States. These tobacco plants are being grown in a field near Winston-Salem, North Carolina.

many years. Add to this the fact that no new smoker intends to smoke a pack or more a day for the rest of his or her life. However, this is exactly the result for many people because nicotine is one of the most addictive substances that exists.

CASE STUDY

Jeanine is a 58-year-old married woman living in Pontiac, Michigan, with her husband, Norm. Norm and Jeanine both smoke a pack of cigarettes a day and have done so since their youth. Norm started smoking in middle school. Jeanine started smoking in her early twenties. Norm is a salesman who works at a furniture store. Jeanine works on the automobile manufacturing assembly line for General Motors (GM). Jeanine was hired by GM right out of high school and moved up from a clerical job to the assembly plant floor within a few years. She earns an excellent salary and has vacation time and benefits.

Jeanine can remember when everyone in the plant smoked, and all of their smoke breaks were taken indoors. Once, there were even cigarette vending machines in all the break rooms. Back in those days, no one thought about quitting.

Norm and Jeanine both smoke a cigarette first thing in the morning, before breakfast. They make coffee, read the paper, eat some eggs and sausage, then have a few more cigarettes before they leave for work. Jeanine smokes another couple of cigarettes during her half-hour drive to work.

Things have changed at GM. As newer staff members have been hired, fewer smokers are left, although there still are plenty of employees who smoke. But now smoke breaks have to take place outdoors, and employees get only one 15-minute break every 4 hours. Jeanine uses both of her breaks, plus her lunch hour, to smoke 8–10 cigarettes. Then she smokes 2–3 more on her way home, another few after dinner, and a few more before bed. The next day, the cycle starts all over again.

Jeanine has tried to quit smoking many times in the past. Sometimes, she would make it for several days or even weeks before succumbing again. Usually, it was Norm's continuous smoking that would encourage Jeanine to start smoking again. Norm enjoys smoking and sees no reason to quit. When Jeanine brings up the issue of health, Norm points to his 91-year-old father, who still smokes and is relatively healthy. So, for the last few years, Jeanine hasn't tried to fight her addiction. She continues to smoke right alongside her husband.

But things are gnawing at Jeanine. She feels she is out of shape physically, and she gets winded doing even light exercise. In addition, she occasionally gets a twinge of pain in her chest when she's exerting herself. This scares her, but she is afraid to go to the doctor to get it checked. Her father died of a heart attack at 62 and her mother died of cancer at age 70. Now there's also pressure at work to develop a healthy lifestyle. GM is holding free health clinics to help employees lose weight, eat properly, and quit smoking. The company advertises that it will provide free smoking cessation treatment. Jeanine is strongly considering signing up for this program.

Jeanine's story provides a good example of society's changing views toward cigarette smoking. Once a common activity, it was even prescribed by doctors for complaints like anxiety or stress. People in the 1960s and 1970s could smoke in virtually every public place, including airplanes. A sea change occurred in the latter part of the twentieth century as smoking was banned in more and more places. Some states, such as New York and California, have banned smoking in all public areas.

Jeanine started smoking with her friends and later developed her addiction to the point of daily use, including when she was alone. It is not unusual to see people with this history. Efforts to quit are stymied by friends or family who continue to smoke. Cigarettes are silent killers—health problems usually aren't noticed until they are very advanced. Jeanine has been diagnosed with **hypertension**, or high blood pressure, which can be caused by or made worse by smoking. She also may have symptoms of coronary artery disease, as evidenced by her

Figure 4.2 Emphysema is a painful disease of the lungs that makes it very difficult for the person affected to breathe. This is a picture of the lung of a person who has died of emphysema. The large blackened spots are cavities in the lung lined with heavy deposits of carbon.

chest pain. This is another condition that is worsened by cigarettes. In addition, she has a family history of cancer, which puts her at a much higher risk for developing cancer herself—a disease that is definitely linked to cigarettes and other forms of tobacco.

HOW NICOTINE AFFECTS THE BODY

Nicotine works by stimulating brain cells and increasing how often they send signals. The effects of nicotine last a relatively short time; its half-life in the blood is about 30 minutes. This is one reason why chronic smokers have to smoke all day long. They are, in essence, trying to maintain a constant level of nicotine in their bloodstream.

The short-term effects of nicotine include increased alertness, energy, and enhanced memory. Nicotine is also said to ease tension and stress and decrease the appetite. Some side effects include a quickened pulse and higher blood pressure. Nicotine can also aggravate asthma and cause anxiety and insomnia.

The long-term effects of nicotine (especially in people who have used it for 10 or more years) include hardening of the arteries, called **atherosclerosis**, all over the body, including the heart. In addition, smokers have a much higher risk of **strokes**, heart attacks, **emphysema**, lung cancer, bladder cancer, and mouth and throat cancer.

People do not usually **overdose** on nicotine but it is possible in theory. The symptoms of an overdose would be a racing heart, sweating, tremor, intense anxiety, weakness, nausea, **seizures**, and ultimately death. Another danger, however, is when nicotine is taken in combination with a different stimulating drug, such as cocaine. The effect of the two drugs together can cause severe **vasoconstriction** of the arteries around the heart and potentially cause a heart attack.

OTHER DANGERS OF SMOKING

Nicotine use during pregnancy can lead to many complications, including a higher chance of miscarriage and low fetal birth weight.[13]

Secondhand smoke has only recently been found to be a health hazard for nonsmokers. Findings related to the health risks associated with secondhand smoke provide the foundation for restrictions on smoking in hospitals, airplanes, restaurants, and other places where children, sick persons, or the general public could be exposed. While a smoker usually inhales smoke through the filter of a cigarette, others in the area breathe the unfiltered fumes of burning tobacco. People who live with a smoker or work in a smoky environment are most at risk. A

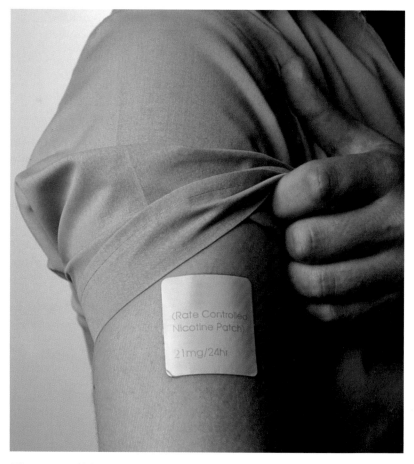

Figure 4.3 Although quitting smoking can be very difficult for people who are addicted to nicotine, there are many ways to help people quit, including nicotine replacement patches like this one, which help decrease the severity of withdrawal symptoms.

recent study showed that over 10 years, regular exposure to secondhand smoke *doubled* a person's risk of heart disease. This adds up to more than 50,000 heart attacks per year that can be attributed to secondhand smoke exposure.[14] Furthermore, there is some evidence that secondhand smoke plays a role in **sudden infant death syndrome** (**SIDS**).

TREATMENT FOR NICOTINE ADDICTION

The smoking cessation industry is a multibillion-dollar business. At any given time, millions of smokers are trying to quit. There are numerous ways to help those who cannot quit alone. One strategy is to utilize the principle of "strength in numbers." The camaraderie of quitting with a friend or family member can be helpful for many people who try to quit smoking. For others, a nicotine-substitute product can help ease the withdrawal symptoms and cravings that occur with smoking cessation. Nicotine gum, lozenges, and patches are available for this purpose (and can be dangerous if used along with tobacco products). A smoker can also ask a physician for help in the fight to quit smoking, using certain medications, like Zyban® or another **psychotropic** medication. The aid of a psychologist or counselor may also help the person identify the mental states or behaviors that lead to and contribute to smoking, so that they can be changed. One simple strategy is to avoid people and places that trigger the urge to smoke. Hypnotherapy has also been useful for some people in the fight to quit smoking.

Finally, education is very important. This education should not only cover the health risks of tobacco and nicotine, but also the biology of nicotine addiction—such as the fact that nicotine cravings, though intense, usually last for only three to five minutes. If they can be overcome, it may be hours or days before another craving hits.

Next, we will look at alcohol—another widely used and highly addictive (but legal) drug.

5 Alcohol and Other Sedatives

DEFINITION OF ALCOHOL ADDICTION

Alcohol dependence is the medical term for alcohol "addiction," or alcoholism. Alcoholism is one of the most pervasive and serious addictive disorders in the United States. The costs associated with treating alcoholism and the medical conditions that result from it are $50 billion per year. In addition, because alcoholism can take a toll on a person's ability to function at a job, alcoholism costs the United States over $100 billion a year in lost productivity.

For the purposes of this chapter, we will be grouping a class of drugs known as **sedatives** with alcohol, since sedatives have many of the same effects and addictive qualities. Most sedatives are prescription medications given for insomnia, seizures, or anxiety. They include such medications as diazepam (Valium®), alprazolam (Xanax®), and lorazepam (Ativan®). Abused sedatives that are illegal substances include gamma-hydroxybutyrate (GHB) and methaqualone (quaaludes).

THE HISTORY OF ALCOHOL USE

Alcoholic beverages are commonly associated with celebrations, religious observances, and recreation in cultures throughout the world. The ancient Greeks and Romans drank alcohol for both recreation and medicinal purposes but also advocated moderation in its use. With the spread of Christianity, excessive use of alcoholic beverages for recreation was discouraged and a more sober lifestyle was promoted. However, the use of alcohol became common throughout western European society with an increase in the popularity of the distillation of alcohol in the twelfth and thirteenth centuries. **Distillation** is the process of purifying and concentrating alcohol. Since water and alcohol have different boiling points, heating the mixture to a certain temperature will separate the two. Alcohol boils first and leaves the boiling brew as a vapor. This vapor is collected and distilled spirits are the result.

A fermented mash of grain may be 15–20% alcohol, whereas distilled spirits are 70–90% alcohol. The growing popularity of distilled alcohol brought with it a higher rate of addiction to alcohol and the problems associated with it. Accordingly, new laws were passed to help reduce the rates of drunkenness. By the late fifteenth century, the sale of alcohol in Germany was prohibited on Sundays and religious holidays. Germany was also the first nation to start the **temperance** movement. Temperance refers to moderation or self-restraint in the use of alcohol. This philosophy is still common throughout much of the world today.

Benjamin Rush (1745–1813), a Philadelphia physician known for signing the Declaration of Independence and as the father of American psychiatry, believed that alcohol consumption had negative health effects and that addiction to alcohol was a disease. In 1787, Rush published an essay called "An Enquiry Into the Effects of Spiritous Liquors Upon the Human Body, and Their Influence Upon the Happiness of Society." He went on to propose ways to deter people from buying and using alcohol. For his efforts, he is considered the founder of the American temperance movement. Between 1825 and 1840, the consumption of distilled alcohol in the United States fell by 75%.

Jerry is a 27-year-old band manager who lives and works in Nashville, Tennessee. He grew up in a home where no one drank alcohol. He was told that alcoholism runs in his family. His grandfather was an alcoholic who died from liver cancer, a consequence of his lifelong addiction to alcohol. When he was younger, Jerry thought he would live a life of abstinence like his father had. However, he had his first drink in college. At first, he believed drinking was no big

Prohibition in the United States

In 1919, the manufacture, sale, and transportation of alcohol was prohibited by the 18th Amendment to the Constitution of the United States. This legislation was enacted as a direct response to the growing problem of alcoholism in the United States. Prohibition, on some level, was effective. The average consumption of alcohol dropped from 2.6 gallons (9.8 liters) per person per year to under 1 gallon (3.8 liters) per person per year. In addition, alcohol-related deaths and arrests decreased. The flip side of Prohibition was that it gave rise to a black market for alcohol, which was often controlled by organized crime. Many politicians and police officers were bribed to allow the underground alcohol establishment to flourish. Illegal bars, called speakeasies, popped up in which people could buy and drink alcohol. Prohibition lasted 14 years. In the end, it was repealed because American citizens felt that restricting alcohol consumption was overreaching by the U.S. government and because many believed that the law was ineffective and unenforceable. The 18th Amendment was repealed by the 21st Amendment in 1933, which granted individual states the right to regulate their own alcohol industry.

deal, certainly not the evil force that his family had portrayed it to be. Jerry thought his alcohol use was normal among his peer group—he consumed three to six drinks when he went out and occasionally binged, drinking up to a dozen shots at fraternity parties. After graduation, he began to manage musical acts for the country-music industry in Nashville. He noticed that his pattern of drinking remained constant, since he had to entertain clients and spend a lot of time hanging out in the bars where his clients performed. Within two years, he found that he was drinking even when he was alone, both at bars and at home. He tried to stop drinking and found that he was a nervous wreck and couldn't sleep. He realized that these symptoms vanished when he had a couple of drinks, and that he needed alcohol in his system to avoid such unpleasant symptoms. He also realized that he was addicted to alcohol. Over the next couple of years, his drinking continued at a moderate daily pace. He made two trips to the emergency room during this time for abdominal pain. At the first evaluation, he was asked about his alcohol consumption and he lied, saying he rarely drank. He was diagnosed with acid reflux and sent home. The second time he went to the emergency room, he was in a lot more pain and was diagnosed with pancreatitis, an inflammation of the pancreas often caused by excessive alcohol use. During that visit, the emergency room doctor confronted him about his drinking and Jerry admitted that he had been drinking at least four to six drinks every day.

Jerry's personal life had deteriorated. He didn't have many good friends and hadn't had a steady girlfriend in four years. He was also slipping at his job. Sometimes he wouldn't show up for his clients' performances or wouldn't schedule new ones for them. He would get to work late and sometimes wouldn't show up at all. He knew he had a problem and that

Figure 5.1 Alcohol addiction causes more than just physical problems. It can lead to depression and the loss of friendships, which can cause a person to feel isolated.

he needed help. During a phone call with his parents, he broke down in tears and told them about his alcohol addiction. His parents drove up within days of the call and took him to an alcohol and drug treatment center.

Jerry was detoxified from alcohol over seven days, using medications to suppress his withdrawal symptoms. Then he started to take part in behavioral therapy groups while he was still at the recovery center. He was transferred to a residential treatment center for three weeks and was released when he earned his one-month sobriety chip from Alcoholics Anonymous (AA). He plans to attend daily AA meetings for the next two months. He is also in the middle of a career switch, so he can remove himself from the daily proximity to alcohol. He has obtained an entry-level marketing job with an entertainment company, which requires office meetings with corporate clients rather than long evenings in smoky bars with musicians.

Like many addictions, Jerry's problem began with casual use that grew out of control over time. Jerry entered his addiction with the knowledge of his family history of alcoholism. Yet, like most addicts, he thought he would be able to control his alcohol use. Jerry did meet the criteria for addiction—alcohol

Alcohol Dependence Questionnaire[15]

The following simple four-question test can help health-care providers screen for individuals who may be addicted to alcohol:

1. Have you ever felt the need to cut down on your drinking?
2. Have you ever felt annoyed by someone criticizing your drinking?
3. Have you ever felt guilty about your drinking?
4. Have you ever felt the need for an eye-opener (a drink first thing in the morning)?

If the person answers yes to two or more of these questions, he or she may have a problem with alcohol addiction.

dependence. He showed increasing use of a substance that caused him both physical illness and social and occupational dysfunction. His life was becoming unmanageable because of his excessive use of alcohol.

HOW ALCOHOL WORKS

Alcohol works by enhancing the function of the neurotransmitter **gamma amino butyric acid** (**GABA**). GABA is the main **inhibitory** neurotransmitter in the brain. It is responsible for such things as calming and drowsiness. If GABA is enhanced, then neurons become less active. Alcohol may also reduce the effect of **glutamate** (the primary **excitatory**

Levels of Intoxication*

1–3 drinks ** over 1 hour:**
(blood alcohol content reaches up to 100 mg/100 ml***)
- decrease in anxiety and stress
- lowering of inhibitions
- pleasure/mild euphoria
- increased sociability

3–6 drinks over 1 hour:
(blood alcohol content reaches between 100–300 mg/100 ml)
- dizziness
- loss of coordination
- poor memory
- difficulty standing or staying awake
- nausea and vomiting
- slurred speech

neurotransmitter), thereby working in two ways to slow down the brain's activity.

THE EFFECTS OF ALCOHOL ON THE HUMAN BODY

Even occasional use of alcohol during pregnancy can be harmful to the fetus. Babies born to women who engage in moderate to severe alcohol use may exhibit **fetal alcohol syndrome.** This condition, in its most serious form, causes physical deformities and mental retardation in the newborn. The safest option for a pregnant woman is to not drink any alcohol at all, since no safe level has ever been determined.

Alcohol overdose is a serious matter. Thousands of people,

6–12 drinks over 1 hour:

(blood alcohol content reaches 300–600 mg/100 ml)

- **hypothermia or hyperthermia (body temperature that is too low or too high)**
- **unresponsiveness with no movement**
- **shallow breathing**
- **can lead to death**

* Keep in mind that different people react differently to alcohol and that many factors determine what effects alcohol will have on a given person. Some factors include the amount of alcohol use in the past, age, and body weight. This list is just a guide.

** One drink is defined as 0.6 ounce (17.7 ml) of alcohol, the amount typically found in 12 ounces (355 ml) of beer, 5 ounces (148 ml) of wine, or 1.5 ounces (44.4 ml) of distilled liquor

*** The blood alcohol content considered by most states as "Driving While Intoxicated" begins between 80 and 100 mg/100 ml

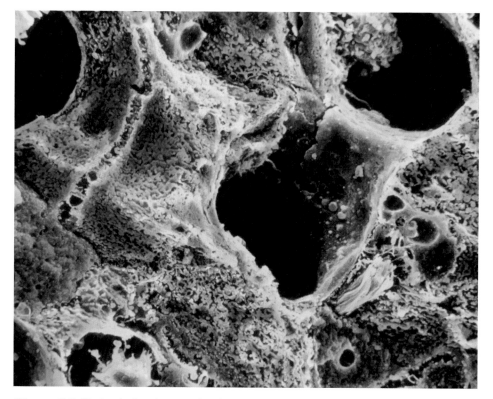

Figure 5.2 Cirrhosis hardens and enlarges the liver until the organ can no longer function properly. In this colored photograph, liver cells surround blood-carrying channels (blue), while phagocytes (yellow) associated with tissue damage are seen in these channels.

including adolescents, die of alcohol overdose or **alcohol poisoning** every year. It doesn't take much hard liquor to kill a human being, especially one who is not used to drinking alcohol. Common causes for alcohol poisoning are heavy drinking on an empty stomach or playing drinking games. The risk is even greater when alcohol is combined with other substances that have similar effects, such as sedatives like Valium or other drugs that cause drowsiness. Signs of alcohol overdose include nausea and vomiting, disorientation, slowed breathing, and unresponsiveness.

Using alcohol heavily over a long period of time can result in serious physical damage. Long-term effects include shrinkage of the brain, **cirrhosis** (hardening) of the liver, a weakened and enlarged heart, malnutrition, impotence and low sperm count in men, stomach ulcers, pancreatitis, and easy bruising and bleeding. It is also associated with an increased occurrence of certain cancers of the liver, mouth, throat, esophagus, and stomach. In addition to the obvious physical effects, depression of mood is often a side effect of alcohol abuse.

The liver is especially susceptible to damage from alcohol abuse over time. The liver works to **detoxify** the blood in the human body. Large amounts of any toxin, including alcohol, introduced to the body over a long period of time place tremendous stress on liver function. The liver breaks down alcohol using a series of enzyme reactions. Heavy alcohol use increases the risk of developing cirrhosis of the liver. This can progress to the point that the liver can no longer function. People who have this problem may need medical or surgical intervention, and sometimes a liver transplant may be necessary.

TREATMENT

The treatment of alcohol addiction was the first recognized and formalized addiction treatment. For those people who truly meet the definition of alcohol dependence, the best first step to obtain treatment is a complete medical and psychiatric evaluation. Alcohol withdrawal is one of the most dangerous forms of drug withdrawal. In its severe form, known as **delirium tremens**, or DTs, a person may experience the sensation of bugs crawling on the skin, hallucinations, agitation, dangerously high blood pressure and pulse (to the point of causing a heart attack or stroke), hyperthermia, seizures, and even death. DTs are a medical emergency and the treatment must take place in a hospital setting to help stabilize the person's cardiovascular and central nervous system. Even when full-blown DTs do not occur, people who give up even moderate levels of alcohol intake may experience the "shakes" (tremors), insomnia, agitation, high blood pressure and pulse, and irritability. When in doubt, it is always best to consult with a health-care professional if any of these serious symptoms take place.

The window for developing withdrawal is within the first three to eight days of sobriety. This is the extremely difficult part. But each day after that can be just as difficult in another way—resisting the temptation to drink again. Most addictions are lifelong diseases, which means that, to avoid a relapse, a person *must remain sober for life.* Even one drink can lead to a complete relapse with consequences just as treacherous as before. This is why experts say that recovery from an addiction must happen one day at a time.

There are treatment tools that can help with this process. Any underlying psychiatric disorder, such as depression or an anxiety disorder, should be treated by a health-care professional. Even in the absence of such disorders, individual therapy may be utilized to help the patient break out of the cycle of addiction. There are now medications available to help treat some addictions, like alcoholism. These will be discussed in more detail later. One of the most popular and successful forms of treatment includes the 12-step group process, known as Alcoholics Anonymous.

Alcoholics Anonymous

Most people in the United States have heard of the treatment program known as Alcoholics Anonymous, or AA for short. AA was the first organized treatment program in the United States for any sort of addiction. It was founded in Akron, Ohio, in 1935, by a surgeon named Bob Smith and a stockbroker named Bill Wilson. Both men were alcoholics. Wilson had stopped

The 12 Suggested Steps of Alcoholics Anonymous

1. We admitted we were powerless over alcohol—that our lives had become unmanageable.
2. We came to believe that a power greater than ourselves could restore us to sanity.
3. We made a decision to turn our will and our lives over to the care of God as we understood him.
4. We made a searching and fearless moral inventory of ourselves.
5. We admitted to God, to ourselves, and to another human being the exact nature of our wrongs.
6. We were entirely ready to have God remove all these defects of character.
7. We humbly asked God to remove our shortcomings.
8. We made a list of all the persons we had harmed, and became willing to make amends to them all.
9. We made direct amends to such people wherever possible, except when to do so would injure them or others.
10. We continued to take personal inventory and, when we were wrong, we promptly admitted it.
11. We sought through prayer and meditation to improve our conscious contact with God, as we understood him, praying only for knowledge of his will for us and the power to carry that out.
12. Having had a spiritual awakening as the result of these steps, we tried to carry this message to alcoholics, and to practice these principles in all our affairs.

Source: ALCOHOLICS ANONYMOUS: The Story of How Many Thousands of Men and Women Have Recovered from Alcoholism, 2nd ed., 1955.

drinking and stayed sober by working with other recovering alcoholics. Both men started to work with other alcoholics at a local hospital. They described a path to recovery from alcohol addiction that consisted of 12 steps. Although the steps did not subscribe to a particular religion, they did involve spirituality as part of the recovery process. By 1939, there were three groups in Ohio that had helped 100 alcoholics stay sober. A Cleveland newspaper published stories about the groups and AA membership exploded. By 1950, 100,000 alcoholics around the world had used AA's philosophies to get sober and stay sober. One of those recovering alcoholics, Marty Mann (the first woman to use AA to achieve sobriety), founded the National Committee for Education on Alcohol, now known as the National Council on Alcoholism and Drug Dependence (NCADD). NCADD was instrumental in the latter half of the twentieth century in helping to change the way the public views alcoholism. What was once considered a moral failing or lack of willpower became, thanks in part to the educational campaign of NCADD, considered a disease.

Because of the success of AA, sister groups have developed, such as Narcotics Anonymous (NA) for drug dependence of other kinds. NA uses the same 12 steps from AA's philosophy, but substitutes the word *addiction* for *alcohol*. Because of the anonymous nature of AA and NA, and the fact that no records of meetings are kept, it is hard to obtain hard data on the numbers of people involved or the success rate. What is known, however, is that tens of thousands of groups hold weekly or even daily meetings in more than 100 countries around the world, helping alcohol and drug addicts stay sober, one day at a time.

There are also support groups for the family members of alcoholics. Lois Wilson, wife of one of the founders of AA, created Al-Anon, and later, the teenage son of an alcoholic founded Alateen. The mission of these groups is to provide strength and hope to people who live with an alcoholic.

Marijuana

6

THE HISTORY OF MARIJUANA

The cannabis plant originated in central Asia and is now one of the most lucrative cash crops in the world. The leaves and flowering tops of these plants are referred to as **marijuana.** People have known about marijuana's mind-altering qualities for thousands of years. The earliest reference to the drug is found in archaeological evidence in China dating back 12,000 years. The psychoactive compound in marijuana is **delta-9-tetrahydro-cannabinol (THC).** Marijuana plants can vary in their THC content from 1% to 7%. **Hashish** is the more concentrated resin of the cannabis plant. It is a stronger drug than marijuana, with a THC content of up to 10–20%. The term *hashish* comes from the Arabic word for "grass." *Grass* and *weed* have become other popular terms used for marijuana.

The cannabis plant came to be very useful during the Renaissance, especially through the sixteenth century. Grown as hemp, it was a great source of material for rope, fabric, and paper. In fact, at one point in the sixteenth century, the British government ordered farmers to grow hemp because it was useful in supplying the navy with sails for ships. The utility of hemp continued until cotton came to be the dominant fiber in the New World.

By 1900, there were more than 30 marijuana-derived compounds available commercially for medical use, produced by

Figure 6.1 Marijuana, which is made from the cannabis plant (seen here), has been used as a drug for thousands of years.

several pharmaceutical companies. However, by the nineteenth and early twentieth centuries, worries about side effects such as impotence and sterility caused concerns about marijuana use. The 1937 Marijuana Tax Act made cannabis illegal in the United States. Before the 1960s, marijuana use was fairly limited—only 3% of the population between the ages of 18 and 25 had used it. By 1970, however, this percentage had increased to 40% of those between the ages of 18 and 25, and by 1980, usage was even more common. Today, usage has declined; only 5% of the general population regularly uses marijuana.

CASE STUDY

Brian, a 20-year-old college student, was arrested for the possession of marijuana, which was discovered when he was stopped by police for unsafe driving. He was charged with driving under the influence of cannabis, and his license was suspended.

Brian was first introduced to marijuana by his girlfriend, who uses it every day, and whose mother also uses marijuana.

Ancient and Historical Uses of Marijuana

- A "food of the gods" in ancient India
- Used as a medicine in China to relieve pain and cure ailments
- Zulu warriors in Africa smoked marijuana prior to battle
- Human sacrifices were given marijuana to prepare them for death
- African Bashilange tribes gave marijuana to criminals as a "truth agent" to encourage them to confess
- Japanese women burned marijuana to drive away evil spirits
- Used in Japanese wedding ceremonies to promote monogamy
- Used in medieval Europe to hasten the wedding day of young women
- Used in Ireland to help a woman foretell her future husband
- Used in Iran to achieve spiritual insight

Later medicinal uses have been to ease menstrual discomfort and the pain of childbirth, and marijuana had been prescribed for such things as depression, cough, jaundice, inflammation, tumors, arthritis, gout, venereal disease, incontinence, cramps, insomnia, epilepsy, alcohol withdrawal, and asthma.

Brian initially smoked just with his girlfriend and her mother, but within six months, he began to use it on his own because he thought it helped him handle the stress of college. Now Brian smokes both alone and with friends; however, sometimes he would not use marijuana for weeks at a time, especially when he was being closely watched by his parents. Brian introduced his 17-year-old brother to marijuana, but his brother felt paranoid when he tried it and has not smoked since.

Brian is the oldest of three children and continues to live at home while attending college. His mother is a successful attorney and his father is a school administrator. Brian has

Medical Marijuana

Since 1996, 11 states have passed medical marijuana laws, which make it legal for doctors to prescribe marijuana for their patients. Most prescriptions are given to patients who suffer from chronic pain that does not respond to traditional pain medications. The problem with enacting these laws is that federal drug prohibition preempts state laws and, therefore, state governments are locked in a legal tug-of-war with the federal government. The issue of states' rights versus federal oversight remains a controversial one in the U.S. judicial system. A 2005 U.S. Supreme Court ruling stated that the U.S. federal government can override state law, thus making the growing and distribution of medical marijuana a violation of federal drug laws.

States with Medical Marijuana Laws:

Alaska, Arizona, California, Colorado, Hawaii, Maine, Montana, Nevada, Oregon, Vermont, Washington smoked cigarettes since age 16 and currently smokes one pack a day. He drinks on occasion and has been smoking marijuana several times a week for a year. His usual pattern of use is to go on weekend binges, starting to smoke on Friday evenings and then again early in the day on Saturday, continuing into the evening. He has had two car accidents that occurred while he was under the influence of marijuana.

During recent months, he has occasionally smoked marijuana on school nights as well as weekends. On the mornings after he uses marijuana, Brian tends to sleep in and cut class. Although he has always been a good student, his grades have begun to drop and he is not fulfilling his academic potential; he has also limited his recreational and social interests. Brian's parents detected his use of marijuana six months ago, and since that time, Brian has been in a constant struggle with his parents. When his parents first found out about his marijuana use, they insisted that he seek professional help for what they perceived as a drug problem. They even threatened to call his college dean, but Brian still refused help and began to talk about quitting school. He did cut down his marijuana use somewhat, and, when pressed by his parents, he would abstain for several weeks at a time.

Brian admits that since he began to smoke marijuana, his previously good and trusting relationship with his parents has turned sour. He has been hiding his use, has lied to his family, and has felt increasingly negative about himself, especially as his grades have suffered and his general interests have narrowed. He has tried cocaine and LSD once, but he found both experiences unpleasant. It was not until his arrest for possession of marijuana that he decided that drug use was ruining his relationship with his parents and might interfere with his plans to become an attorney. He has also become gradually aware that marijuana may be affecting his motivation and schoolwork.

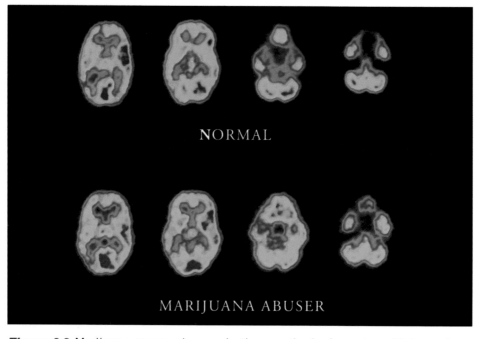

NORMAL

MARIJUANA ABUSER

Figure 6.2 Marijuana causes changes in the way the brain works, which can be seen in a positron emission tomography (PET) scan. In this photograph, the images at top show the brain of a person not under the influence of marijuana, while the images below show the brain of a person who has used marijuana. The color differences indicate changes that make the marijuana user uncoordinated and lead him or her to demonstrate poor spatial judgment.

As a result of his recent arrest, Brian is legally required to seek professional help, in exchange for a lighter punishment for his drug possession. Brian met with a psychiatrist and was diagnosed with dysthymic disorder (a chronic, mild depression) and occasional panic attacks. The doctor started Brian on treatment for these symptoms. Brian is trying to stay off of marijuana, but has occasional relapses. He has a hard time accepting the fact that he may have to end his relationship with his girlfriend, who still uses marijuana, if he wants to stay clean.

Brian's case is compelling. He was introduced to what he thought was a harmless drug and, before long, he became dependent on cannabis and wound up with a police record. Perhaps just as disconcerting is the fact that he may have to end his romantic relationship if he wants to change his life for the better. This case illustrates how some people end up in a situation that helps keep their addiction going. If Brian drops out of therapy and continues to date his girlfriend, he will have little chance of beating his dependence.

EFFECTS OF MARIJUANA

The most common method of marijuana use is by smoking, either in a cigar, pipe, or cigarette. It can also be eaten, where it is usually mixed in with other foods.

All drugs of abuse have a combination of positive and negative effects. The positive effects are the reason people use the drug. The negative effects, however, can be prominent. The short-term effects of marijuana use last between two and eight hours and can include **euphoria**, relaxation, increased appetite, and dizziness. Some side effects include disorientation, poor memory, and distorted vision or hearing. Brian's brother in the example above had a severe side effect—he became paranoid. Some people also experience hallucinations when they take marijuana.

For those people who continue to use marijuana regularly, other effects enter the picture. Many people view marijuana as a benign drug. However, a little-known fact about marijuana is that it does have long-term consequences. Because most users smoke it, one of the long-term dangers is marijuana's effects on the lungs, which are similar to the risks from smoking tobacco. Marijuana has even more dangerous and toxic chemicals in it than cigarettes. This, coupled with the fact that most marijuana smokers tend to inhale more deeply than cigarette smokers and hold the smoke longer in their lungs, makes marijuana even more dangerous than cigarettes. Health risks include bronchitis, emphysema, asthma, and lung cancer. Additional health problems caused by marijuana use are memory loss, depression, sexual dysfunction, and decreased sperm count in men, but these effects are still being studied.

Did You Know?

Interesting Facts About Marijuana in the United States

1. At the time the Declaration of Independence was written (1776), cannabis and hemp were used in:
   - the paper on which the document was written
   - 90% of American clothing
   - the canvases of great paintings
   - the first flags of the United States.
2. Paper made from hemp cannabis is physically superior to that made from wood pulp.
3. Hemp paper is still used for bank notes and archives.
4. Marijuana, though illegal, is the largest cash crop in the United States, with earnings estimated at $32 billion per year.
5. Most marijuana (55%) used in the United States comes from Mexico.
6. Marijuana is the most commonly used illegal drug.
7. The term *pot* comes from Mexican slang—*potiguaya*.
8. Chocolate stimulates some of the same receptors in the brain triggered by marijuana, but to a much, much smaller degree.

IS MARIJUANA ADDICTIVE?

There has been much debate about whether or mot marijuana is addictive. Some medical professionals say it is, while others say it is not. The truth probably lies somewhere in the middle. Although it may not be as addictive for its users as cocaine or nicotine, there are certainly people who turn into compulsive, daily users of marijuana.

For a chronic user of marijuana, the withdrawal symptoms after long-term, heavy use are typically not life-threatening and are milder than those seen with other drugs of abuse or alcohol. Withdrawal symptoms may include insomnia, hyperactivity, decreased appetite, nausea, diarrhea, and restlessness. Sweating, salivation, tremors, and an increase in pulse and temperature may also occur. Furthermore, for some people, withdrawal and abstinence may uncover the original reason they started to use the drug—a mood or anxiety disorder for which they were using marijuana to self-medicate.

OVERDOSE DANGERS

Can people overdose on marijuana? They can, but it is very hard to do. Because the content of THC in smoked marijuana is usually low and the method of burning it is rather inefficient, it is very difficult, if not impossible, to overdose on marijuana by smoking it. Hashish, on the other hand, has a higher THC content and is steadily absorbed through the gastrointestinal (GI) tract when eaten and could potentially cause symptoms of overdose. Having said this, there is no known case of death by marijuana overdose. Some of the symptoms of marijuana overdose would be a low blood pressure, racing pulse, and unresponsiveness.

Ecstasy

THE HISTORY OF ECSTASY

Ecstasy is the street name for an amphetamine compound called methylene-dioxy-methamphetamine, or MDMA. In 1913, the pharmaceutical company Merck created MDMA to be tested as an appetite suppressant, but it failed in animal tests and was never given to human subjects. Forty years later, in 1953, the U.S. government used MDMA in experiments on the effects of psychoactive substances on humans, to see if it had any military uses. It did not. Then, in 1965, an American biochemist named Alexander Shulgin (who had an interest in psychoactive drugs) made MDMA in his laboratory. Ten years later, he published a paper on MDMA's effects on humans and told a psychiatrist friend about it, who began to give MDMA to his therapy clients. It was thought that MDMA had uses in talk therapy because it could help patients relax and open up, and could perhaps help them achieve insight or confront deeply repressed thoughts, feelings, or memories. In the late 1970s and early 1980s, MDMA, now known as Ecstasy, was being discussed at medical conferences for its potential therapeutic benefits. However, laboratory tests demonstrated that MDMA destroyed brain cells in animals. As a result, the U.S. Drug Enforcement Agency (DEA) put MDMA on its list of Schedule I drugs, effectively outlawing it.

Figure 7.1 Dr. Alexander Shulgin, seen here in 2001 in his laboratory, made and studied MDMA, better known as Ecstasy.

Illegal MDMA use has continued to the present day and MDMA has become a popular party drug. Most of the MDMA available illegally today is manufactured overseas. Because MDMA is made in the form of a pill, there is no way to tell if what is claimed to be MDMA actually *is* MDMA. So, in addition to the dangers of taking illegal MDMA, there is the added danger of taking a pill of unknown origin, which could contain any substance, even a lethal one. Many people have used what they thought was Ecstasy, only to wind up in the emergency room or even dead from ingesting a toxic substance.

MDMA in pill form is usually swallowed. However, some people have crushed it and either snorted or injected it.

Figure 7.2 Ecstasy is commonly used by teens and young adults at dance parties called raves. The crowded, often overheated conditions at raves make using the drug even more dangerous.

Although these methods of drug delivery may have faster results, the risks associated with them are severe. Users are exposed to pneumonia (an infection of the lungs) or sepsis (an infection of the blood), not to mention HIV (human immun-odeficiency virus) and other blood-borne diseases if needles are shared.

MDMA has become very popular among high school and college students, and at parties called raves. A recent study by the National Institutes of Drug Abuse showed that around 5% of students between 8th and 12th grades have tried Ecstasy. The popularity of MDMA grew between 1995 and 2002. This is demonstrated by statistics from hospitals that participate in the

Drug Abuse Warning Network (DAWN). These hospitals report that MDMA overdoses or adverse reactions from MDMA have climbed from 400 per year to more than 4,000 per year.

CASE STUDY [16]

Mandy is a 27-year-old graduate student. She describes, in her own words, her experience with using Ecstasy:

All of my friends were doing it, my boyfriend was doing it, and they were all doing it every weekend (or there about) and none of them seemed to have been affected by it and all of them appeared to be having so much fun with the whole thing. They always kept trying to coax me into coming out with them.

My friends and boyfriend said it was fantastic and not to be scared to take it. They explained to me that all the sensations you normally feel are heightened and that it was nothing to be scared of. I asked a lot of questions before I made the choice to try it so that I could know to some extent what to expect. I felt nothing at first then all of a sudden I felt so happy and free. I felt like nothing mattered and that I could take on any situation. It made me feel like I was the best at everything, that breaking up with my boyfriend didn't matter. It made me feel like I could dance and sing for hours upon hours. It made me feel more daring. I felt happy and free. The top of my head felt tingly and I felt very energetic.

The next day and after a fair few hours (after taking it) I felt okay at first. . . . [F]or me, it was a general growing feeling of uneasiness, then feeling as though my thoughts were all over the place. Also feeling myself become less happy and then starting to feel a little anxious. A fair amount of time later, I felt very erratic in my behavior and also felt like I was tired but couldn't sleep. My mind felt like it was racing.

When I looked back at what I did, I felt disgust at myself, as I had always been so against drugs of any kind and I had become a complete hypocrite. Then as well as this I had a frightening experience. One of the pills I took had a bit of trip or acid in it and I started seeing all sorts of shapes. When I looked in the mirror, my face was distorted and I felt my heart racing at a million miles an hour. I couldn't relax and I was terrified because everything I looked at became distorted. When I closed my eyes I saw colors and images of I really don't know what. My hearing also became distorted and I could hear noise like when someone turns the channel on the TV onto a channel with no picture—hissing and buzzing.

I was witness to a person collapsing in front of me. That person collapsed in to an unconscious state, foaming at the mouth, lips went blue and their teeth did not stop chattering. An ambulance was called and they were taken away to a hospital. I do not know what happened to that person. I also knew a guy who died. He was a friend of a friend. He died in his sleep and I do know that he had been out taking the Ecstasy drug all weekend, nonstop for two days. He had not been home or slept for 48 hours. He died from choking on his own vomit in his sleep.

The temptation can be so great. So many people around you can appear to be having the best time and having no side effects or aftereffects. But there will be. It may not happen the first time or the second time, but it will have adverse effects on your body. The scariest part is nobody knows if it will affect him or her in the same way as the next person and you do not know what you are taking. The depression and scatterbrain thoughts that can come with taking Ecstasy can be incredibly distressing and if you experience any acid-trips effects or depression, this can be awfully frightening.

There is no definite expected reaction to this drug; that is the scariest part. The temptation can be overwhelming and there may be no problem experienced at all in the beginning. But because it can feel so awesome to some, that is how it becomes addictive. Then the need to have more and more each time to acquire the same sensation grows. The strain on your heart, kidneys, and liver is immense and cannot be underestimated. Also, the fact that you can, without meaning to, over-hydrate yourself. Too much or too little liquid can have dreadful effects. There are way too many unknowns and, though the original thrill and sensation may seem so fantastic, if the ability to look at what it was really doing to the body was apparent, I believe most people would stop immediately and be ashamed at what they had done to their own body. Resist the temptation!

It is evident from Mandy's words that the business of drug abuse is serious indeed. Stories of addiction are all quite similar. Casual drug use escalates to the point of total consumption of a person's thoughts, energies, and resources. Mandy describes becoming a hypocrite—she is someone who originally looked down on drug users, yet she herself became one. She also tells about many of the different reactions that people have to drug use—some are not affected much and others pay the ultimate price, in hallucinations, a trip to the hospital, or even death. She also clearly illustrates how the drug she thought was Ecstasy turned out to be laced with LSD, causing her to have bizarre and unstoppable visual and auditory hallucinations.

EFFECTS OF ECSTASY

The effects of MDMA resemble those of both the stimulants and hallucinogens. In the short term, they can cause euphoria, increased energy, and self-esteem, but they can also alter normal vision and hearing to the point of hallucinations. People like using Ecstasy for its sensory-heightening effects. However, there can be many dangerous side effects of the drug. These may include a loss of appetite, dehydration, rapid pulse, tightening of the jaw, dilated pupils, sweating and fever, confusion, panic attacks, and even severe depression. A real danger exists at rave parties where physical activity (dancing) and dehydration (which occurs with MDMA use) can cause severe hyperthermia or even death. Another indirect effect of the drug is that, due to its lowering of inhibitions, people are more likely to have sex (often unprotected) with strangers. The results of this are not only embarrassment and shame, but a higher risk of sexually transmitted diseases (STDs) and unwanted pregnancies. Mind-altering drugs can lead people to do things they would not consider doing while sober.

LONG-TERM CONSEQUENCES OF USE

People who regularly use MDMA may develop symptoms of psychiatric disorders. Studies with animals have shown that even one dose of MDMA can destroy neurons in the brain. MDMA appears to destroy the nerve terminals of serotonergic brain cells. Serotonin is a chemical neurotransmitter that is critical for normal brain function. Problems with serotonin are associated with psychological disorders that range from anxiety to depression and bipolar disorder.

Researchers have also reported lower performance on memory tests by MDMA users compared with people who do not use MDMA. This is the most significant difference between MDMA and most other illicit drugs: MDMA has the potential to permanently and severely damage brain cells with even casual use. MDMA seems to permanently change the brain with even occasional or light use. Studies into the permanent physical damage resulting from MDMA usage are ongoing. What can be said about MDMA use is that it may lead to higher rates of depression, anxiety disorders, or memory problems later in life. Those people with preexisting psychiatric or **neurological** disorders may be especially affected by MDMA use and should not even experiment with this drug.

Withdrawal from Ecstasy is usually a rebound from the clinical effects that it brings. This means that, within a day or two of use, the user may feel depressed, fatigued, and want to be alone. Users may also experience muscle aches, abdominal pain, chills, tremors, and hunger. Some users even experience a deep depression.

Risk of Overdose

Fatal overdose can occur with MDMA. Overheating of the body is one potentially fatal effect, as a body temperature over 104°F (40°C) can cause brain damage and eventually death. Anyone who experiences symptoms of MDMA overdose needs immediate medical care. Even low doses of MDMA may ultimately be fatal in susceptible individuals (people whose livers cannot break down the drug). Signs of MDMA overdose include fever, confusion, rapid heart rate, agitation, blurry vision, tremor, paranoia, and elevated blood pressure. More severe consequences of overdose may include hallucinations, seizures, stroke, coma, and death.

ADDICTION TO ECSTASY

The addictive potential of MDMA is lower than that of other drugs, scientifically speaking. This does *not* mean that there are not compulsive and regular users of Ecstasy out there. There are. The frightening aspect of this is that, over the next several years, additional evidence will undoubtedly accumulate to confirm how toxic MDMA is to the human brain. Unfortunately, by then, the warning may be too late for some people.

Cocaine and Stimulants

Cocaine and amphetamines ("uppers") belong to the class of drugs called **stimulants**. They get this name because their net effect is to stimulate nerve cells, resulting in increased energy and endurance, improved mood and alertness, and increased attention and memory.

Cocaine comes from *Erythroxylon coca*, an indigenous plant of South America. Natives of the Andes mountains have been eating the coca leaf as a part of their daily diet for thousands of years, and it remains a traditional part of their diet even to this day. Chewing the leaf provides a mild stimulation. The danger and addictive potential comes from cocaine, the concentrated powdered form of the coca leaf, which was first produced in the nineteenth century. At that time cocaine became an ingredient in various tonics throughout western Europe and America, including Coca-Cola®. The rapid rise in cocaine use also resulted in toxic tragedies since merchants would add unregulated amounts to their products. Today, cocaine is a Class II controlled substance—it is only legal for use in certain surgeries as a local anesthetic.

Amphetamine is a stimulant that was made in a laboratory in the early twentieth century, primarily to treat asthma. Later, scientists learned that this medication caused euphoria and a boost in energy, and that it was addictive. Methamphetamine, also made synthetically, is a chemical cousin of amphetamine.

Figure 8.1 The native people of South America, where the coca plant grows, have eaten the plant's leaves as part of their regular diet for thousands of years, as this Bolivian plantation worker is doing.

Crystal methamphetamine, a drug that gets a lot of national attention these days, is also a synthetically formed stimulant that resembles glass, or pieces of crystal. Many states in the United States have a growing problem with the illegal manufacturing of methamphetamine, since it is a homegrown stimulant, made in makeshift laboratories with ingredients that are fairly easy to get. New laws restricting the sale of Sudafed® and other over-the-counter medications that contain pseudoephedrine have helped curtail the rapidly growing methamphetamine trade.

Jim is a 17-year-old high school student living in the Midwest. He comes from a single-parent home. His mother, who cares for him, works two jobs and lets Jim do pretty much as he pleases. One of his friends introduced him to Melissa, a college student who invited Jim and his friends out into the country with her and her boyfriend, Peter. It was here in a house on a quiet country road where Jim first smoked ice, a concentrated form of crystal methamphetamine. With only two puffs, Jim was on cloud nine. He felt incredibly good, as if he didn't have a care in the world. One of Jim's friends refused to try it. Another tried it and felt uneasy and needed to lie down. Jim, on the other hand, made plans to use crystal meth again. He bought some rocks from Peter and Melissa, who make the drug in a trailer in their backyard.

Jim became a regular customer of Peter and Melissa, buying several times a week until his meager savings ran out. Determined to keep up his drug use, Jim agreed to sell crystal meth back at school in exchange for free hits of the drug. Jim's friends were astonished to learn that Jim had become part of the drug trade and refused to hang out with him. Jim didn't care much, since he had his new friends who supplied him with drugs. He could no longer imagine life without crystal meth.

Jim's usage of crystal meth escalated because he developed tolerance. He could never quite achieve the same level of euphoria that he had during his first days of using. He was using crystal meth on a daily basis, sometimes not eating for days. He lost 30 pounds (13.6 kg) and looked as pale as a ghost. His mother suspected that something was wrong but reluctantly accepted Jim's convincing assertions that he was fine.

One day, while smoking crystal meth at Peter and Melissa's house, a convoy of police cars stormed up and surrounded the property. Police officers broke in with guns drawn and arrested everyone present. Jim was shocked. He had never even seen a gun before, let alone been arrested, cuffed, and put in a police car. The drug bust made the local news and identified Jim as a "Monroe County high-schooler." His mother was heartbroken and furious, but she was supportive enough to help her son get an attorney to fight his legal battles.

In police custody, Jim was irritable and depressed as he detoxified from the drug he had been using every day. When he was alone, he felt like the walls were closing in on him and felt that it was difficult to breathe. He never thought he would end up in jail. At the court hearing, Peter and Melissa were set to go to trial since they pleaded not guilty. They each faced 40 years in prison if convicted, since they had a prior history of drug offenses and were charged with manufacturing and distributing crystal meth. Jim's mother and attorney were present at Jim's hearing. Jim pleaded guilty to the charges against him. Because he was a minor and this was his first offense, the judge was lenient and ordered him to go to a drug rehabilitation program, spend two years on probation, and perform 200 hours of community service, teaching young people about the dangers of drug abuse.

The course of Jim's life was drastically changed by his arrest. Because he was caught as a minor, he was able to receive a lighter punishment than his friends and had a chance to turn his life around. Had he been 18, he would have

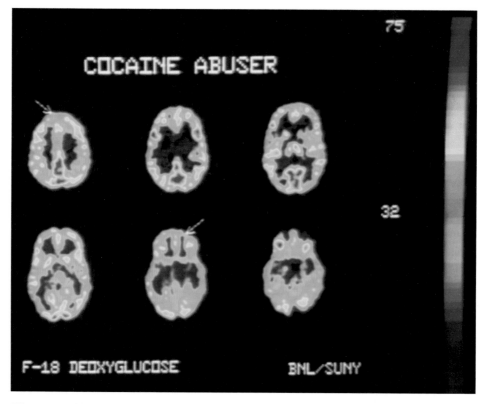

Figure 8.2 Cocaine and other stimulants have dramatic effects on the brain. This PET scan shows how cocaine makes the brain much more active than normal.

been sentenced to two to five years in prison and would have had a record as a convicted felon. Jim's story with meth shows the compulsive use, tolerance, and withdrawal common with drug addiction. His story also shows the personal, physical, and social deterioration that can follow.

Some stimulants, like dextroamphetamine (Dexedrine®, Adderall®) and methylphenidate (Ritalin®) are used as treatments for narcolepsy and attention-deficit/hyperactivity disorder

(ADHD). These stimulants are generally milder than cocaine or methamphetamine, although they can still have some of the same side effects. Plus, the prescription stimulants can also be addictive. All stimulants work through the neurotransmitters **norepinephrine** and **dopamine.** By acting on these two neurotransmitter systems, stimulants allow both chemicals to exert a greater effect in the brain. Stimulants also have a significant effect on the **cardiovascular** system—they elevate heart rate and blood pressure, cause the pupils to dilate, and decrease appetite.

EFFECTS OF STIMULANTS

Stimulants' effects last only for a few minutes to a few hours, depending on the type used. The use of stimulants can cause

Bad Drugs Get Worse

There is no doubt that stimulants like cocaine and amphetamine are potent and dangerously addictive drugs. But people's incessant and sometime reckless pursuit in refining a product has resulted in even more volatile forms of the two drugs: crack cocaine and crystal methamphetamine. These drugs are similar in that they are the rock form of the drug and both are usually smoked, causing a sudden onset of effect, as well as danger. Some researchers have stated that these drugs are so powerfully addictive that even a single use by a susceptible individual can lead to addiction. Many thousands of recovering crack and crystal meth addicts have said the same thing— recounting their experiences from living a normal life to becoming destitute and homeless in a matter of weeks as their addiction spiraled out of control.

increased energy, alertness, endurance, and euphoria. This is why they are often called "uppers." Other effects include a feeling of invincibility that can reach a delusional level (such as leading people to believe they can outrun police). Taken in excess, the stimulants can cause insomnia, weight loss, paranoia, hallucinations, and **panic attacks**. Jim and his friends exhibited some of these side effects. The stimulants can also lead to dangerously high blood pressure, agitation, and violent behavior. Stimulant abusers may suffer heart attacks or strokes because of the stress the drugs put on their cardiovascular system. They can also experience seizures and, ultimately, death.

Addicts' craving for crack cocaine and other stimulants can be so intense that they become willing to do anything to achieve the next high. Unfortunately, sometimes this means that they lie, cheat, and steal. At times, they even are likely to become violent, either as a result of the high or the steep decline from it. In recent years, it seems that the stimulant trade (both cocaine and methamphetamine) has been plagued with violence and destruction more than that of other illegal drugs.

Another major adverse effect of stimulants is the effect of hypersexuality, or increased sexual appetite. This can sometimes lead to sexual assault, promiscuity, contraction of sexually transmitted diseases such as HIV, and unwanted pregnancies. Activation of the dopamine neurotransmitter system is responsible for this. Stimulants can push people into sexual encounters that they would not normally engage in. A subset of new cases of HIV infection has been attributed to crystal meth and other stimulant abuse in group settings, leading to casual and unprotected sex.

Overdose is certainly possible with cocaine, methamphetamine, or other stimulants, and any urban emergency room doctor will tell you that it happens regularly. Overdose typically overloads the cardiovascular and central nervous systems, causing seizures (convulsions), stroke, heart **arrhythmia**, heart attack, and sometimes death. Overdose is especially dangerous when a stimulant is mixed with a sedating drug, like heroin. The sedating drug "takes the edge off" the stimulant's side effects, and the user can accidentally overdose on the stimulant. This is what is believed to have happened to the *Saturday Night Live* comic John Belushi. He died from a drug overdose—both cocaine and heroin were found in his bloodstream.

9

Heroin and Other Opiates

Heroin belongs to a family of chemicals called opioids, or opiates. These are medicinal compounds made from the opium poppy plant. Opiates target **receptors** in the human body that can moderate or ease pain. In fact, the human body has its own opioid compounds, known as **endorphins**. The body releases endorphins in times of intense pain or stress. Common opiates used in medicines today include **morphine**, **codeine**, **hydrocodone**, and **oxycodone**. Heroin is a precursor to morphine—it is converted to morphine inside the body. Oxycontin® (a long-acting form of oxycodone) is another opiate drug that has recently become infamous as a legitimate pain medication that is often abused.

Opiates including heroin were legal around the world until about 100 years ago. As casual and recreational use grew, so did the realization that these drugs had serious and sometimes lethal effects and addictive potential.

Since many opiates are available by prescription for the use of pain, it is no surprise that some people begin their path to addiction with a legitimate prescription. Then, either because of a tendency toward addiction or the cycle of withdrawal associated with these drugs, people can wind up with an opiate dependence. Many people around the world use opiate pain medication on a daily basis. Does this make them addicts? Absolutely not. Remember, the definition of *addiction* involves the escalating use of a substance along with dysfunction at

Figure 9.1 Heroin and other opiate drugs come from the opium poppy plant, seen here.

work, school, or with peers. Chronic opiate use can certainly cause a physical dependence that would lead to withdrawal symptoms if the medication is suddenly stopped, but this alone is not considered addiction.

The common forms of use for the opiates are ingesting by mouth (swallowing pills) or injecting directly into the bloodstream. Heroin is usually injected or smoked. Injecting opiates (or any drug, for that matter) presents a unique danger—related to the use of a dirty needle. The worldwide use of intravenous (IV) drugs has contributed significantly to the global HIV/AIDS crisis.

Blair is an aspiring writer and musician who is 19 years old and lives in Los Angeles, California. He moved there immediately after graduating from high school in the Midwest. His parents wanted him to go to college, but Blair had dreams of becoming a rock star. Blair's father is a high school teacher and his mother is unable to work because of a back injury that causes her severe chronic pain. Blair has a sister who is still in high school.

Blair joined a band called Northstar with other musicians he met in L.A. One of his bandmates, Tim, first introduced Blair to heroin. He told Blair that musicians often use heroin to help the creative process and listed a number of famous musicians who found their niche in music by using it. Blair tried heroin by smoking it since he was afraid of using a needle, and he fell in love with it instantly. Blair found peace and tranquillity in the initial effects of heroin. He felt like he could truly get his mind around ambiguous concepts such as the yearning for love and the meaning of life. His bandmates, however, began to complain about the way he smelled when he smoked heroin. After that, Blair tried to inject with the

Needle-Exchange Programs

A controversial solution to the problem of escalating HIV and hepatitis rates among IV drug abusers is to provide them with free, clean needles. The intent of programs like this is to decrease drug addicts' tendency to share needles and, therefore, lower their risk of contracting or passing on these deadly diseases. Critics have said, though, that by providing free needles, society is inadvertently approving of drug use and even encouraging it. Nevertheless, many large cities in the United States continue to operate needle-exchange programs.

help of his bandmate Tim. He found it relatively easy and still loved the rush he got from the drug.

Blair began to use heroin every day. Soon, it took the place of music in his life. While under its influence, Blair felt at peace, able to solve the mysteries of life in his mind—why bother writing music? His bandmates kicked him out of the band because he "couldn't hold his dope." Without Tim as his supplier, Blair had to go out and find heroin on his own. This took him several days and, each day, he became more anxious and on edge, feeling unable to live without this drug. When he finally located a supplier, he could not even wait until going home to shoot up. He injected himself right there in the car and passed out for two hours. A police officer spotted him drooling in the car and investigated. The officer called for an ambulance when Blair was unresponsive. The officer spotted a needle on the floor of the car and suggested to medical personnel that it may be a drug overdose.

Upon arrival at the emergency room, Blair was given **naloxone**, an antidote for opiate overdose. Within minutes, he woke up and became agitated, not knowing where he was or how he got there. He began to yell at a nurse that the hospital owed him $100 because they took away his "heroin high." The nurse called a psychiatrist to evaluate Blair.

Two years later, Blair lives with the realization that he has a heroin addiction and that he is powerless over it. After several unsuccessful attempts to stay clean on his own, he enrolled in a methadone maintenance program. Methadone is a pain medication that also functions as a heroin substitute. A special clinic gives Blair two days' worth of methadone at a time, and he sees a psychiatrist routinely. He attends Narcotics Anonymous meetings regularly. Blair has given up music for a while and now works three part-time jobs to make ends meet.

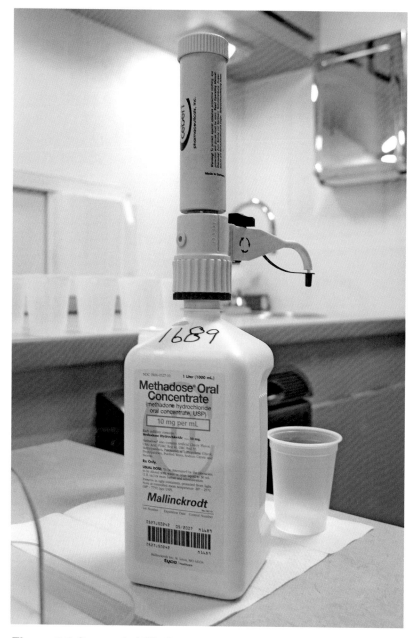

Figure 9.2 Some rehabilitation centers use the drug methadone to help ease the cravings of recovering opiate addicts.

EFFECTS OF OPIATES

The effects of opiates at low to moderate doses include sleepiness, pain relief, and a feeling of tranquillity or bliss. Side effects at these doses include itching, constriction of the pupils, and constipation. At higher doses, confusion, slurred speech, clammy skin, a drop in blood pressure, slowed heartbeat, and shallow breathing can result. Overdose can lead to unresponsiveness and death.

The commonly used antidote available for opiate overdose is **naloxone** (Narcan®). It is stocked in every hospital in the United States. It almost immediately reverses all of the opiates' effects on the body. It has this life-saving effect by displacing the drug from the millions of opiate receptors throughout the body. Many lives have been saved with this antidote.

Heroin Overdose

Heroin and other opiates have contributed to many premature deaths since this class of drugs has existed. Heroin overdose takes the lives of thousands of people every year in the United States. The lives of many more are ruined by the power of this addiction. One example is rock musician Janis Joplin. Joplin was a blues-influenced rock singer whose career rose to great heights in the late 1960s—one of her biggest hits was "Piece of My Heart." After attending college in Texas, she moved to northern California, where she joined the music scene and experimented with drugs and alcohol. Her addiction became an on-again, off-again pattern for her. In 1970, she accidentally died of a heroin overdose at the age of 27.

WITHDRAWAL SYNDROME

Opiate withdrawal, as recovering addicts will tell you, is probably the worst experience known to humankind. Although it is not life-threatening, opiate withdrawal can cause many intense symptoms, such as a sharp increase in pain and anxiety, flu-like symptoms (runny nose, watery eyes), vomiting, diarrhea, fast pulse rate, elevated blood pressure, dilated pupils, coughing, and severe muscle cramps. The emergence of goose bumps and clammy skin during opiate withdrawal gave rise to the term *cold turkey*, which means to abruptly stop the use of a drug. The intensity of withdrawal from opiates is one of the reasons why opiate addiction is so hard to break—the user desperately tries to cure the withdrawal symptoms by using more of the drug.

TREATMENT FOR OPIATE ADDICTION

Heroin and opiate addiction can be notoriously difficult to overcome. People who are addicted are likely to fail multiple attempts at achieving sobriety. Many of the typical treatments for opiate addiction are the same as for other addictions: sobriety, 12-step support groups, individual therapy, and the treatment of any underlying psychiatric disorders. However, there are also unique treatments for this addiction, the primary one being **opiate maintenance treatment** (like the methadone maintenance discussed in Blair's story).

The concept behind opiate maintenance treatment is to provide enough biological activity of an opiate drug to quell the withdrawal and cravings in opiate-addicted individuals without providing the pleasurable effects of opiate abuse and dependence. Methadone is the most common drug used in maintenance programs. It is an opiate medication meant to be taken once a day. The addictive potential, though still present, is much less than that of heroin or other shorter-acting opiates. Patients are screened for any current drug use by urine and blood tests. If they are clear of all drugs and alcohol, they are started on methadone on a very strict basis—at first, they are only given one day's supply at a time so that there is no possibility for abuse. LAAM (levo-alpha-acetyl-methadol) and buprenorphine are two other opiate compounds used as opiate maintenance treatments in the recovery process.

Opiate maintenance programs are sometimes the only way for certain patients to break the cycle of opiate addiction. These programs are sometimes controversial, however, since not everyone agrees with the idea of giving an opiate addict more opiate substances. Studies show, however, that if they are monitored correctly, these programs can be successful. All opiate maintenance treatments operate under strict governmental controls.

10 Inhalants and Hallucinogens

Two unique drugs in the spectrum of addiction are inhalants and hallucinogens. Both of these categories of drugs do not seem to have the same properties of addiction shared by the other drugs we have discussed so far. They seem to be used solely for their mind-altering properties. There is little, if any, tolerance, dependence, or withdrawal associated with inhalants or hallucinogens. Nevertheless, they are dangerous for the effects they can have and the actions that can result.

INHALANTS

It has only been in the last century or so that manmade chemicals and solvents were introduced into the marketplace. **Inhalant** abuse (also known as **huffing** or **sniffing**) has become another method of mind-alteration. Substances such as gasoline, kerosene, paints, solvents, and glues are typically used in this activity. Some of the effects of inhalants include visual hallucinations, a sense of exhilaration, skin sensitivity, lowering of inhibitions, and giddiness. The user may also experience lightheadedness, dizziness, confusion, disorientation, and drowsiness. The dangers of overdose from inhalants include brain damage (death of neurons, especially in the **cerebellum**); injuries to the face, mouth, throat, and lungs; burn injuries; irregular heartbeat; slowed breathing; lack of coordination; confusion; coma; and even death.

Figure 10.1 Inhalant abuse, often called "huffing," is a serious problem, especially among children and teenagers. This boy is using a plastic bag to concentrate fumes as he inhales them.

Inhalants can be very toxic because most of them are not meant for human ingestion. There are three broad categories of inhalants: **nitrites, anesthetics,** and **solvents**. Nitrites are flammable chemicals that are deadly if swallowed and can cause lethal burns. Solvents are the most dangerous ones to inhale (or swallow): They are poison. Solvents are chemicals that can lead to **"sudden sniffing death"** by causing heart arrhythmia. Some of the chemicals can also catch fire while being sniffed, causing burn injuries. Refrigerants can cause a drop in skin and mucous membrane temperature so severe that **frostbite** and death have been reported. One study showed that of all inhalant deaths, 20% occurred in first-time users. Inhalants are perhaps the most dangerous drugs of abuse, yet their easy availability makes them very common among adolescents. A truly frightening statistic is that 8% of middle-schoolers and more than 15% of high school seniors report having used inhalants at some point.

Dr. Timothy Leary

Timothy Leary was born in 1920 and became a writer, psychologist, and 1960s-era proponent of LSD. Having used the drug himself, Leary became an advocate for the use of LSD and other hallucinogens as recreational drugs, but also as forms of treatment for conditions like alcoholism and criminality. Leary's views were controversial and not very popular with the government—former president Richard Nixon called Leary "the most dangerous man in America." In 1963, Leary and a colleague, Dr. Richard Alpert (who shared Leary's views), were dismissed from their duties as Harvard University for conducting research on graduate students on the effects of psilocybin and LSD.

A decade later, Leary's practices caught up with him. He was arrested for possession of marijuana in 1972. He spent some time behind bars but escaped from prison and fled the country. Two years later, he was caught abroad and extradited back to the United States. In a surprise twist, he was pardoned in 1976 by then–California governor Jerry Brown. Leary spent the rest of his life writing and touring the country. He died in 1996.

HALLUCINOGENS

Hallucinogens are drugs that throughout history have been considered the most "**psychedelic**" because they cause the greatest distortion of reality. The best-known example is **lysergic acid diethylamide**, or **LSD**. Others include **peyote, psilocybin, phencyclidine** (PCP), and ketamine. LSD was very popular among recreational drug users in the 1960s. Its use declined until about 1986, when its use started to increase again. By the end of the twentieth century, approximately 10% of high school seniors across the country had reported trying LSD.

The biological effects of hallucinogens include visual and auditory illusions (distortions) or hallucinations, and a feeling of departing from reality. They can also speed up or slow down the sense of time. They work by affecting serotonin in parts of the brain. Some of the unpleasant effects can include confusion, disorientation, depression, fear, and panic. The signs of LSD or hallucinogen overdose can be fever, rapid pulse, high blood pressure, drooling, muscle rigidity, paranoia, mutism, agitation, and pressured (rapid and continuous) speech.

One of the greatest dangers of hallucinogens is that the distortion of reality and hallucinations which come with their use can cause people to do unpredictable things. Someone high on LSD may feel as if they can fly and jump off a building. Or they may feel that a friend is actually a mortal enemy and take violent action against them. It is this impairment of judgment and reasoning caused by these drugs that puts users of hallucinogens at great risk for legal trouble, harm, or even death.

Non-Drug Addictions: Food, Sex, and Gambling

Our current classification system includes the use of only ingestible psychoactive substances as addictions. There has been much research and speculation about various other behaviors that are often described as addictions. Some of these include addictions to food, sex, gambling, and even such things as shopping and the Internet. It forces us to ask: What are these conditions? Are they simple acts of overindulgence? Are they a lack of self-control? Or are these non-drug addictions partly biologically based phenomena that represent illness rather than personal failure? Although this notion has been sensationalized in pop culture and media, the truth lies somewhere in the middle. Let's take a look at three non-drug compulsions that have been described as addictions by the medical community for at least half a century.

PATHOLOGIC GAMBLING

For some people, the act of rolling dice, pulling the lever on a slot machine, playing the lottery, or betting on a poker match involves a thrill like no other. Some of these people may have a compulsive gambling habit that leads to personal and financial ruin. The thrill of gambling rises above all else. These people may have a condition known as pathologic gambling. The DSM-IV definition requires an individual to meet 5 of

Figure 11.1 For some people, the thrill of gambling can become an addiction that leads to severe financial and personal problems.

the following 10 criteria, and not be in the midst of a manic episode (a feature of bipolar disorder):

- is *overly preoccupied* with gambling
- needs to gamble with *increasing amounts* of money
- has *unsuccessfully* tried to stop
- becomes *restless* or *irritable* when trying to stop
- gambles to *escape problems* or relieve depression

- tries to get *even* with previous losses from gambling
- *lies* about the extent of gambling
- has *committed illegal* acts to finance gambling
- has *lost a relationship or job* due to gambling
- or *relies on others to provide money* for financial assistance due to gambling losses

Any one of these criteria may indicate that a person's gambling behavior is excessive. However, for a diagnosis of pathologic gambling (gambling addiction), at least five of them must be present.

When pathologic gambling is diagnosed, it is easy to see how closely it resembles drug addiction. There is compulsive engagement in the activity, tolerance to it that requires "higher doses," and a huge personal cost to sustain the activity. One study found that, in some gamblers, the level of natural endorphins—the human body's tranquillity agent—was reduced compared with non-gambling subjects.[17] This leads to the hypothesis that those people who may be susceptible to pathologic gambling are biochemically different from others and may use gambling as a way to feel more normal.

BINGE-EATING DISORDER

Binge-eating disorder can be considered an addiction to food. It consists of compulsive binges on food, even when there is no hunger or need for food. Like a drug addict, a binge eater will try to hide his or her behavior and usually engages in it when alone. The definition of binge-eating disorder includes recurrent episodes of binge eating, which is defined as eating larger than normal amounts of food within a two-hour period along with the feeling that this is uncontrollable. Other features necessary for the diagnosis are eating more rapidly than normal, eating until uncomfortably full, eating when *not* feeling hungry,

Figure 11.2 Binge-eating disorder is a form of food addiction in which the person eats massive amounts of food within a short period of time, even when he or she is not hungry.

eating alone because of embarrassment, and feeling disgusted, depressed, or guilty by the subsequent bingeing. If there is **purging** associated with the bingeing, then perhaps a diagnosis of another eating disorder, such as **bulimia nervosa**, needs to be considered.

Although someone with binge-eating disorder may or may not be overweight, one of the medical ramifications of this condition is its impact on the health. Overeating can contribute to and cause obesity, diabetes, and hypertension (high blood pressure). This can result in heart attacks, strokes, and other negative health consequences.

SEXUAL ADDICTION

The concept of a person engaging in compulsive sexual activity to the point of breaking moral codes, relationship covenants, and even the laws of society is a controversial topic. Many members of the public, including health-care professionals, have questions and doubts about this condition—indeed, it is not a condition that is currently listed as a psychiatric disorder in the DSM-IV. Inappropriate or excessive sexual behavior is perceived to be one of the greatest failures of personal discipline. Although some may think this addictive "disorder" is less serious than others, the first case of such a condition was reported over 100 years ago by German psychiatrist Richard von Krafft-Ebbing:

> to such an extent that it [sex] permeates all his thoughts and feelings, allowing no other aims in life, tumultuously, and in a rut-like fashion demanding gratification without granting the possibility of moral and righteous counterpresentations, and resolving itself into an impulsive, insatiable succession of sexual enjoyments. . . . This pathological sexuality is a dreadful scourge for its victim, for he is in constant danger of violating the laws of the state and of morality, of losing his honor, his freedom and even his life.[18]

Just as a food or drug addiction can impact the sufferer's health, so can a sexual addiction. Engaging in compulsive sexual activity can greatly increase a person's risk of unwanted pregnancies and acquiring sexually transmitted diseases such as syphilis, herpes, and HIV. Although sexual addiction treatment programs are not as widespread as other recovery programs, treatment is available. A vast network of 12-step support groups exists all over the United States. In addition, more and more mental health-care professionals are now specializing in the treatment of this condition.

WHAT DO WE MAKE OF THESE CONDITIONS?

It all goes back to the addiction circuit. Many of the activities that humans find pleasurable bring a sense of positive reinforcement in this area of the brain. Could it be that, for some people, the normal pursuit of pleasure escalates or turns into an addiction because of a problem in the circuit in the brain? Studies that are being done on pathologic levels of eating, sexual activity, and gambling have all shown preliminary data that these behaviors have similarities to addiction.[19]

The neurotransmitter dopamine is probably not alone in its involvement in these compulsive behaviors. Another neurotransmitter, serotonin, is believed to be involved in the impulsivity that goes along with excessive alcohol consumption, and, therefore, may play a role in other compulsive behaviors.[20] People who exhibit non-drug addictions have different serotonin "circuits" involved in their activities of compulsion. Of course, this does not mean that anyone who has ever overeaten or engaged impulsively in sex or shopping is an addict. However, as we learn more about these "addictive" disorders, we may be categorizing compulsive eating, gambling, and sex right next to alcoholism and cocaine addictions.

12 Treatment and Recovery

When referring to addicts, people often say, "Why can't they just stop?" Another frequent comment is, "I can stop at two drinks, why can't they?" It is human nature to apply our own sensibilities and judgment to the problems and situations of others. To understand addiction, however, requires out-of-the-box thinking. For most adults of legal age, drinking alcohol is a reasonable, moderated, recreational thing to do. It is an activity within the grasp of the brain's ability for restraint. For a true addict, the need to drink enters the addiction circuit in the brain and is equated with survival.

STEP 1: TREATMENT OF WITHDRAWAL

The first step toward recovery for an addict is to stop using. But even doing this may be a challenge because of the emergence of withdrawal symptoms. In certain cases and with certain drugs, withdrawal symptoms are part of the cycle that keeps people addicted. To break this cycle and to provide a safe method of **detox**, medical treatment of withdrawal symptoms may be necessary. There are certain withdrawal syndromes that can be highly distressing, and some can even be life-threatening without medical treatment. These withdrawal syndromes arise from heroin/opiates, alcohol, and sedatives. The first one is the most uncomfortable. The latter two can be life-threatening.

Table 12.1 Medications Used for Treatment of Withdrawal

ADDICTION	DRUG USED
Alcohol	diazepam (Valium®) or similar drug
Sedatives	phenobarbital
Heroin and other opiates	clonidine

Treatment often consists of inpatient treatment in a specialized hospital setting, often a psychiatric hospital. This treatment can take anywhere from one to five days. Patients' vital signs are closely monitored and they are given medications to ease their withdrawal symptoms.

In addition to these medications, patients are given comfort medications such as non-narcotic pain relievers, cold medicine, anti-diarrheals, and anti-nausea drugs.

STEP 2: DIAGNOSIS AND TREATMENT OF UNDERLYING PSYCHIATRIC DISORDERS

An important next step, preferably carried out at least one month after sobriety, is for the patient to undergo a thorough psychiatric examination. The aim is to figure out why the addiction took place or why it got out of hand. This may reveal some insights into the causes of the addiction and help the person understand his or her own disease. Some people become addicted because they are with the wrong crowd at the wrong time and they have the wrong genes. For others, the situation can be more complicated. People may be trying to self-medicate their untreated psychiatric symptoms. For example, someone going through a major depression may resort to cocaine or some other stimulant to improve his or her mood. A person who suffers

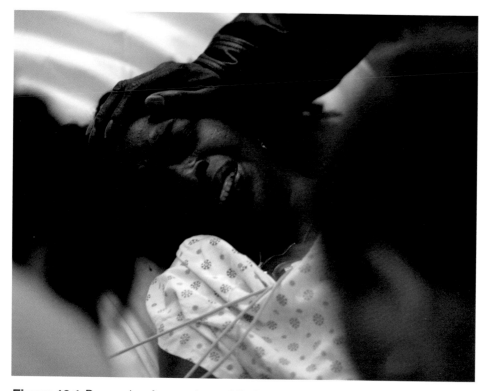

Figure 12.1 Recovering from a drug addiction can be a very difficult and painful process. This woman is going through withdrawal from narcotics at a hospital in San Francisco, California.

from panic attacks may find relief in alcohol, which acts as a sedative. Finally, someone who is suffering from the auditory hallucinations of schizophrenia may use heroin because it helps quell the voices he or she hears. It is vital to identify any psychiatric illness and properly treat it if one exists; otherwise, any efforts at sobriety will ultimately be futile.

STEP 3: COMPLETE ABSTINENCE

Complete **abstinence** is necessary for the treatment of addiction. For an addict, there is no such thing as moderation—it's an all-or-nothing phenomenon. Some people who try to moderate their use of the addicted substance will find themselves back on the slippery slope to addiction.

This requires a multifaceted approach. There have to be major behavioral changes. The patient may need to avoid the people and places that trigger him or her to use the addictive substance. Often, for more severe addictions, this has to be done with the help of a mental health professional. Psychotherapy may be needed during the process of recovery. This usually means regular (often weekly) meetings with a therapist to address behavioral changes required to stay sober, stop having distorted thoughts (such as "no one will like me if I stop drinking"), and address any psychiatric symptoms that may be present. Finding ways to reduce stress and conflict are also essential. Therapy may be individual or may be done in groups of up to 10 with one therapist.

12-STEP SUPPORT GROUPS

Support groups were the first formalized treatment for addiction. Many treatment programs recommend or require alcoholics to attend 90 meetings in 90 days after getting sober. This reinforces the notion of recovery, helps the addict develop a kinship with fellow addicts in recovery, and establishes a commitment to recovery. Addiction is a serious disease that has to be fought one day at a time.

Thanks to the success of AA, numerous similar groups have been formed to help people with all sorts of addictions and compulsive behaviors. Some of these groups include Narcotics Anonymous, Overeaters Anonymous, Sex Addicts Anonymous, and Spenders Anonymous. The list goes on and on. There are even support groups for the family members of addicts, such as Al-Anon and Alateen. For people who may be dissuaded from utilizing 12-step programs because of their use of spiritual principles, there are other, secular groups in existence, like the Secular Organization for Sobriety (SOS).

MEDICAL INTERVENTIONS FOR ADDICTION

A lot of medical science has focused on the disease of addiction over the past 20 years. As we have learned more about addiction as a disease, scientists have developed medications that can aid the patient's process of sobriety and recovery from addiction. What many of these medications do is to help cut down on cravings for certain drugs. Most of them work by affecting the neurotransmitter systems of the brain. These medications are not 100% effective, but they may be helpful for certain individuals. As with most medications, there can be

Table 12.2 Medications Used to Maintain Sobriety

MEDICATION	ACTION
disulfiram (Antabuse®)	Blocks an enzyme necessary to metabolize alcohol— causes the individual to become physically sick and naseous with any alcohol consumption
naltrexone (Revia®)	Blocks opiates from their receptors—useful to break the addiction circuit for alcohol; unproven for other drugs
acamprosate (Campral®)	Affects the neurotransmitter GABA; cuts down on alcohol craving
bupropion (zyban®)	Provides very mild dopamine stimulation; cuts down on tobacco craving
nicotine patch and gum	Nicotine substitution products that help wean individuals off of smoked or chewed tobacco
methadone (Dolophine®)	Opiate substitution that is necessary in some people to reduce craving
buprenorphine	Medication for opiate dependence, considered "methadone-light"

Figure 12.2 Some addicts are able to stay away from drugs by engaging in yoga, meditation, and other relaxation techniques.

certain side effects and risks to taking them. Deciding whether to use medication should be done with the help of a medical professional.

OTHER TREATMENTS

There are a host of different strategies to achieve sobriety. Each affected person may take his or her own individual approach. Some useful strategies include relaxation techniques, **yoga**, **meditation**, **hypnotherapy**, **acupuncture**, and even specific religiously oriented programs.

RELAPSE

No matter how hard a recovering addict tries, there will be a strong temptation to use again. Many addicts go through one or more relapses before they are able to stay sober. Statistics show that between 50 and 75% of people in recovery from the most addictive drugs (alcohol, cocaine, nicotine, and opiates) will relapse within the first year of sobriety.

The message is that if they don't succeed the first time, they should try again. Persistence, as with most worthy goals, is the key to achieving success. With millions of people in the United States and around the world battling these diseases, addiction is not something to be faced alone.

1. The National Center on Addiction and Substance Abuse at Columbia University. *Behind Bars: Substance Abuse and America's Prison Population* New York: CASA, 1998, p. 8.
2. Paul M. Gahlinger, "Flesh of the Gods or the Devil's Poison?," *Illegal Drugs: A Complete Guide to Their History, Chemistry, Use and Abuse.* Las Vegas: Sagebrush Press, 2001, pp. 3–16.
3. Substance Abuse and Mental Health Services Administration *Overview of Findings from the 2003 National Survey on Drug Use and Health.* Rockville, MD: U.S. Department of Health and Human Services, Substance Abuse and Mental Health Services Administration, Office of Applied Studies, 2004, pp. 1–9.
4. E. V. Varga, "The Molecular Mechanisms of Cellular Tolerance to Delta-opioid Agonists. A Minireview." *Acta Biologica Hungarica* 54 (2003): 203–218.
5. Roy A. Wise, "Cognitive Factors in Addiction and Nucleus Accumbens Function: Some Hints From Rodent Models." *Psychobiology* 27 (1999): 300–310.
6. David C. S. Roberts, Karen Brebner, Michelle Vincler, and Wendy J. Lynch, "Patterns of Cocaine Self-Administration in Rats Produced by Various Access Conditions Under a Discrete Trials Procedure," *Drug and Alcohol Dependence* 67 (2002): 291–299.
7. Amanda J. Roberts, Charles J. Heyser, Maury Cole, Peter Griffin, and George F. Koob, "Excessive Ethanol Drinking Following a History of Dependence: Animal Model of Allostasis," *Neuropsychopharmacology* 22 (2000): 581–594.
8. R. D. Spealman, B. Lee, S. Tiefenbacher, D. M. Platt, J. K. Rowlett, and T. V. Khroyan, "Triggers of Relapse: Nonhuman Primate Models of Reinstated Cocaine Seeking," *Motivational Factors in the Etiology of Drug Abuse. Volume 50 of the Nebraska Symposium on Motivation,* ed. Michael T. Bardo and Rick A. Bevins. Lincoln, NE: University of Nebraska Press, 2004, pp. 57–84.
9. Roy W. Pickens, Dace S. Svikis, Matt McGue, David T. Lykken, et al., "Heterogeneity in the Inheritance of Alcoholism: A Study of Male and Female Twins," *Archives of General Psychiatry* 48 (1991): 19–28; Prescott, Carol A., and Kenneth S. Kendler. "Genetic and Environmental Contributions to Alcohol Abuse and Dependence in a Population-based Sample of Male Twins." *American Journal of Psychiatry* 156 (1999): 34–40; Marc A. Schuckit, "New Findings on the Genetics of Alcoholism," *Journal of the American Medical Association* 281 (1999): 1875–1876.
10. John I. Nurnberger, Jr., Ryan Wiegand, Kathleen Bucholz, Sean O'Connor, Eric T. Meyer, Theodore Reich, John Rice, Marc Schuckit, Lucy King, Theodore Petti, Laura Bierut, Anthony Hinrichs, Samuel Kuperman, Victor Hesselbrock, and Bernice Porjesz, "A Family Study of Alcohol Dependence: Coaggregation of Multiple Disorders in Relatives of

Alcohol-Dependent Probands," *Archives of General Psychiatry* 61 (2004): 1246–1256.

11. Duncan B. Clark, Jack R. Cornelius, Levent Kirisci, and Ralph E. Tartar, "Childhood Risk Categories for Adolescent Substance Involvement: A General Liability Typology," *Drug and Alcohol Dependence* 77 (2005): 13–21.

12. Centers for Disease Control. *Women and Smoking: A Report of the Surgeon General.* Atlanta: U.S. Department of Health and Human Services, Centers for Disease Control, 2001, pp. 14–15.

13. National Cancer Institute, "Health Effects of Exposure to Environmental Tobacco Smoke: The Report of the California Environmental Protection Agency," *Smoking and Tobacco Control Monograph No. 10*, ed. Lauren Zeise. Bethesda, MD: U.S. Department of Health and Human Services, National Institutes of Health, National Cancer Institute, 1999, p. 361.

14. Centers for Disease Control, *The Health Consequences of Smoking: A Report of the Surgeon General.* Atlanta: U.S. Department of Health and Human Services, Centers for Disease Control, 2004, pp. 577–600.

15. John A. Ewing, "Detecting Alcoholism: The CAGE Questionnaire," *Journal of the American Medical Association* 252 (1984): 1905–1907.

16. Girl.com/Femail.com Australia, "Ecstasy Case Studies," *Girl.com/Australia.* Available online at http://www.girl.com.au/ cr-ecstasy.htm.

17. Alex P. Blaszczynski, Simon W. Winter, and Neil McConaghy, "Plasma Endorphin Levels in Pathological Gambling." *Journal of Gambling Behavior* 2 (1986): 3–14.

18. Richard von Krafft-Ebbing, *Psychopathia Sexualis.* New York: Arcade Publishing, 1998, pp. 23–464.

19. Mark S. Gold, Kimberly Frost-Pineda, and William S. Jacobs. "Overeating, Binge Eating, and Eating Disorders as Addictions," *Psychiatric Annals* 33 (2003): 117–122; Martin Plant, and Moira Plant, "Sex Addiction: A Comparison With Dependence on Psychoactive Drugs," *Journal of Substance Use* 9 (2003): 260–266.

20. William J. McBride, E. Chernet, J. A. Rabold, L. Lumeng, and T. K. Li, "Serotonin-2 Receptors in the CNS of Alcohol-Preferring and Nonpreferring Rats," *Pharmacology Biochemistry and Behavior* 46 (1993): 631–636.

Abstinence—The act of refraining from the use of a certain item or engaging in a certain behavior.

Acetylcholine—An excitatory protein substance found throughout the body and brain that functions as a signal for nerve cells.

Acid trip—Slang term for the period of intoxication from the substance known as lysergic acid diethylamide (LSD).

Acupuncture—A Chinese form of treatment in which specific areas of the body are pierced with fine needles to bring about a therapeutic effect.

Addiction—The compulsive overuse of a substance that continues in the face of negative and even catastrophic consequences to the user's life.

Addiction circuit—The pathway of nerve cells in the brain that regulates pleasure, which is theorized to go awry during addiction; involves the nucleus accumbens.

Alcohol—An intoxicating liquid that develops over time, consisting of yeast, sugar, and grain.

Alcoholism—Synonymous to alcohol dependence, or addiction to alcohol use.

Alcohol poisoning—An intentional or accidental overdose of alcohol that can prove fatal.

Amphetamine—A medication or illicit drug classified as a stimulant, which works by increasing the activity of nerve cells; also known as speed.

Analgesics—Drugs that help relieve pain.

Anesthetics—Medications used to alleviate pain or alter consciousness; primarily used in medical procedures,

Angel dust—Slang term for phencyclidine (PCP), an illicit hallucinogen.

Arrhythmia, cardiac—An abnormal rhythm of the heart that can cause dizziness, fainting, loss of consciousness, or even death.

Atherosclerosis—The process of hardening of the arteries, which is responsible for heart disease and heart attacks, among other medical complications.

Binge-eating disorder—A psychiatric disorder characterized by eating excessive amounts of food, even when not hungry.

Bipolar disorder—A psychiatric mood disorder characterized by alternating episodes of mania, or pathologically elevated mood, and major depressive episodes; was formerly known as manic depression.

Bronchitis—Inflammation of the bronchi in the lungs, usually due to an infection.

Bufotenine—An illicit and poisonous hallucinogen found on the skin of certain toads or in certain mushrooms.

Cannabis—The plant from which marijuana is derived.

Cardiovascular—Pertaining to the heart and circulatory system of blood vessels.

Cerebellum—The posterior part of the brain that is responsible for coordination and balance.

Chloroform—A poisonous chemical solvent that is sometimes used as an inhalant.

Cirrhosis—A hardening of the liver caused by alcoholism that can be fatal.

Cocaine—A product of the coca plant that acts as a stimulant.

Codeine—An opiate narcotic that is available only by prescription.

Concordance rate—A statistic used in the study of genetics that is the rate at which the same trait is found in a pair of twins.

Delirium tremens (DTs)—A severe alcohol withdrawal syndrome that can cause tremors, disorientation, hallucinations, and cardiovascular abnormalities, and can be fatal.

Delta-9-tetrahydrocannabinol (THC)—The main psychoactive compound found in cannabis, marijuana, and hashish.

Detox (detoxify)—To rid the body of a toxic substance.

Distillation—The process by which alcohol is boiled to separate it from water, resulting in a more concentrated form.

Dizygotic—Pertaining to two zygotes; a reference to twins of the fraternal (nonidentical) type.

Dopamine—An excitatory or inhibitory protein substance found throughout the body and the brain that functions as a signal for nerve cells; it is involved in the perception of pleasure in the brain.

Down-regulation—The process by which a human cell can self-regulate its functioning by decreasing a facet of its physiology, such as by decreasing the concentration of chemical messenger receptors on its surface.

Ecstasy—A special type of amphetamine that also has hallucinatory properties; its full name is methylene-dioxy-methamphetamine (MDMA).

Emphysema—A lung disease that causes a stiffening of lung tissue; often caused by years of smoking tobacco products.

Endorphin—A natural substance, similar to opiates, produced by the body to decrease the sensation of pain.

Euphoria—Intense joy or happiness.

Excitatory—Referring to something that excites or stimulates nerve cells.

Fermentation—The process by which a mixture of sugar, grain, and yeast, becomes alcohol over time.

Fetal alcohol syndrome—Condition that can afflict babies born to mothers who abused alcohol while they were pregnant; it can cause mental retardation and physical deformities.

Freon—A refrigerant that is a poisonous chemical solvent, sometimes used as an inhalant.

Frostbite—The process of cell death due to exposure to extremely cold temperature.

Gamma-amino butyric acid (GABA)—An inhibitory protein substance found throughout the body and the brain that functions as a signal for nerve cells.

Glutamate—An excitatory protein substance found throughout the body and the brain that functions as a signal for nerve cells.

Glycine—An inhibitory protein substance found throughout the body and the brain that functions as a signal for nerve cells.

Hallucination—A sensory perception that exists only in the mind, not in reality; can affect any of the senses.

Hallucinogens—Illicit substances that can cause hallucinations and a distorted sense of time, place, or reality.

Hashish—A concentrated resin of the cannabis plant.

Hemp—A fiber used for paper, clothing, and other goods that comes from the cannabis plant.

Heroin—An illicit drug classified as an opiate narcotic that is similar to the medication morphine.

Huffing—A slang term for the illicit use of inhalants.

Hydrocodone—An opiate narcotic available by prescription as pain medication.

Hypertension—The medical term for the condition known as high blood pressure.

Hyperthermia—Condition in which the body temperature rises too high.

Hypnotherapy—A form of treatment using hypnosis to achieve a therapeutic benefit, such as staying sober from drugs or alcohol.

Incidence—The frequency of the occurrence of a disease.

Illicit—Illegal.

Ingestion—Taking something into the body.

Inhalant—Any substance that can be abused by inhaling; examples are nitrites, anesthetics, and solvents.

Inhibitory—Referring to something that inhibits or slows down nerve cells.

Intoxication—The state of being under the influence of a mind-altering drug.

Ketamine—An anesthetic that has hallucinogenic properties.

Kidney—The organ that exists as a pair in the body to filter the blood and create urine.

Lithium—A naturally occurring salt that is used as a mood-stabilizing treatment for bipolar disorder.

Liver—The bodily organ that functions to rid the blood of toxins absorbed from the stomach and intestines.

Lysergic acid diethylamide (LSD)—A hallucinogenic drug derived from the ergot fungus.

Manic episode—A mood episode lasting at least a week, characterized by elevated mood, increased energy, hyperactivity, decreased need for sleep, flight of ideas, and impulsivity; is more severe than a hypomanic episode; usually representative of bipolar disorder; also known as mania.

Marijuana—A leaf from the cannabis plant that is abused by either smoking or eating; also spelled *marihuana*.

Meditation—A devotional exercise consisting of clearing the mind and remaining still and silent; thought by some to have use as an aid to sobriety from drugs and alcohol.

Methanol—A poisonous chemical solvent that is sometimes used as an inhalant.

Methylene-dioxy-methamphetamine (MDMA)—See Ecstasy.

Methylphenidate (Ritalin®)—A prescription stimulant used to treat narcolepsy and attention-deficit/hyperactivity disorder; it can also be abused.

Monozygotic—Pertaining to one zygote; a reference to identical twins.

Morphine—An opiate narcotic pain medication available by prescription; chemically very similar to heroin.

Myelin—Fatty tissue that surrounds the axons of nerve cells and allows for faster conduction of signaling.

Naloxone (Narcan®)—A medication used as an antidote to opiate overdose; reverses the biological effects of opiates.

Needle-exchange program—A program designed to help reduce the transmission of diseases such as HIV and hepatitis by providing free and clean needles to individuals who abuse drugs by injecting them.

Neurological—Pertaining to nerve cells.

Neuron—A nerve cell.

Neurotransmitter—A protein substance used by nerve cells to signal each other.

Nicotine—The main psychoactive substance in tobacco that has a stimulating effect on nerve cells.

Nitrites—Flammable chemicals that can be abused as an inhalant; can be very dangerous due to the risk of fire and severe burns.

Nitrous oxide—An anesthetic used today by dentists that can be abused as an inhalant; also known as laughing gas.

Norepinephrine—An excitatory protein substance found throughout the body and the brain that functions as a signal for nerve cells; involved in the regulation of various aspects of mood.

Nucleus accumbens—A group of nerve cells in the brain that primarily communicates using the neurotransmitter dopamine; the location of action of several drugs such as amphetamine and cocaine; it is the site where pleasure is experienced and is implicated in the development of addiction (and is the site of the addiction circuit).

Opiate maintenance treatment—Treatment of individuals addicted to opiates involving the administration of small, regular, controlled doses of opiates to help the individuals maintain sobriety.

Opiates—Any of a class of compounds derived from opium, the fluid from the bulb of the poppy plant.

Opium—The milky white fluid from the bulb of an opium poppy plant that has narcotic and addictive qualities.

Overdose—An excessive dose of a substance, whether intentional or accidental, that can have harmful and even lethal effects.

Oxycodone—A prescription narcotic medication classified as an opiate.

Pancreatitis—A painful and severe inflammation of the pancreas that can be a complication of chronic alcohol use.

Panic attack—A severe anxiety state defined by a combination of racing pulse, quick and shallow breaths, chest pain, perspiration, nausea, vomiting, dizziness, and a fear of impending doom.

Paranoia—An over-heightened sense of persecution or distrust of others.

Pathologic gambling—A psychiatric disorder characterized by compulsive gambling in the face of serious negative consequences; akin to a gambling addiction.

Peyote (mescaline)—A hallucinogen derived from a cactus, which is still used in Native American religious rituals.

Phencyclidine (PCP)—A hallucinogen that was originally produced as an anesthetic but is now an illicit drug.

Physical dependence—A facet of addiction that indicates the adaptation made by the body to a drug resulting in physical symptoms if the drug is stopped.

Psilocybin—A hallucinogenic drug derived from mushrooms.

Psychedelic—Characterized by distortions of perception or altered states of awareness; also a slang term for the hallucinogen class of illicit drugs.

Psychiatric—Referring to mental health, mental functioning, or the medical specialty that treats mental illness.

Psychoactive—Referring to something that alleviates fear, elevates mood, eases anxiety, causes an alteration of perception or changes one's state of awareness.

Psychological dependence—A facet of addiction that refers to cravings.

Psychotherapy—A form of treatment that involves using psychological techniques through communication to help identify symptoms and conflicts, change behaviors, and improve overall functioning.

Psychotropic—Refers to a medication or substance that has psychoactive effects.

Purging—In psychiatry, to cause an evacuation of the stomach or bowels; used in reference to an eating disorder.

Receptor—Highly specific protein structure located throughout the body that initiates biological activity when stimulated by a specific substance such as a hormone, drug, or neurotransmitter.

Refrigerant—A poisonous chemical solvent that is sometimes used as an inhalant; an example is freon.

Rush—Slang term for the rapid onset of intoxication from a drug.

Schizophrenia—A psychiatric disorder characterized by dissociation from reality, delusions, and hallucinations.

Secondhand smoke—Smoke that is breathed in by individuals other than the primary smoker.

Sedative—Any of a class of drugs determined to be depressants; these drugs can be illicit or prescriptions that slow down the activity of nerve cells and have an effect similar to alcohol.

Seizure—A neurological event that occurs due to excessive electrical activity in the brain and can cause muscular convulsions, staring spells, and loss of consciousness.

Sexual addiction—A disorder of compulsive sexual behavior with severe negative consequences that is theorized to be similar to other addictions.

Sniffing—See Huffing.

Solvent—A type of poisonous chemical compound abused as an inhalant.

Speed—Slang term for a stimulant such as amphetamine.

Stimulant—An illicit or prescription drug that causes stimulation of nerve cell activity.

Stroke—A disruption of the blood supply to part of the brain caused either by bleeding or a blood clot; can cause paralysis and speech impediments, most of which are permanent.

Substance dependence—The medical term for *addiction*.

Sudden infant death syndrome (SIDS)—A fatal syndrome that affects babies less than a year old in which they stop breathing during sleep; it is thought that secondhand smoke can contribute to this syndrome.

Sudden sniffing death—A fatal event caused by a sudden heart arrhythmia during abuse of an inhalant.

Tolerance—A reduction in biological effect of a drug over time with prolonged use.

Toluene—A poisonous chemical solvent that is sometimes used as an inhalant.

Tranquilizer—See Sedative.

Up-regulation—The process by which a human cell can self-regulate its functioning by increasing or amplifying a facet of its physiology, such as by increasing the concentration of chemical messenger receptors on its surface.

Vasoconstriction—The constriction of blood vessels that usually causes an increase in blood pressure.

Withdrawal—The biological and mental readjustments that have to occur when the regular use of a drug is discontinued.

Yoga—A mental and physical practice of exercise to train the consciousness for a state of perfect spiritual insight and tranquillity, and to promote control of the body and the mind; it may be a useful practice for some people to achieve sobriety from drugs or alcohol use.

American Psychiatric Association. *Diagnostic and Statistical Manual of Mental Disorders,* 4th ed. Washington, DC: American Psychiatric Press, 2000.

Ebert, Michael H., Peter T. Loosen, and Barry Nurcombe. *Current Diagnosis & Treatment in Psychiatry.* New York: Lange Medical Books/McGraw-Hill, 2000.

Gahlinger, Paul M. *Illegal Drugs: A Complete Guide to their History, Chemistry, Use and Abuse.* Las Vegas: Sagebrush Press, 2001.

Holmes, Ann. *Psychological Effects of Cocaine and Crack Addiction.* Philadelphia: Chelsea House Publishers, 1999.

Kaplan, Harold I., and Benjamin J. Sadock. *Synopsis of Psychiatry,* 8th ed. Baltimore: Williams & Wilkins, 1998.

Kuhn, Cynthia, Scott Swartzwelder, and Wilkie Wilson. *Buzzed: The Straight Facts about the Most Used and Abused Drugs from Alcohol to Ecstasy,* 2nd ed. New York: W. W. Norton & Company, 2003.

Lowinson, Joyce H., Pedro Ruiz, Robert B. Millman, and John G. Langrod. *Substance Abuse: A Comprehensive Textbook,* 3rd ed. Baltimore: Williams & Wilkins, 1997.

Peacock, Nancy. *Drowning Our Sorrows: Psychological Effects of Alcohol Abuse.* Philadelphia: Chelsea House Publishers, 2000.

Sadock, Benjamin J., and Virginia A. Sadock. *Kaplan & Sadock's Comprehensive Textbook of Psychiatry,* 7th ed. Philadelphia: Lippincott Williams & Wilkins, 2000.

Stern, Theodore A., and John B. Herman. *Psychiatry Update & Board Preparation.* New York: McGraw-Hill, 2004.

FURTHER READING

DiClemente, Carlo C. *Addiction and Change: How Addictions Develop and Addicted People Recover*. New York: The Guilford Press, 2003.

Goldstein, Avram. *Addiction: From Biology to Drug Policy*. New York: Oxford University Press, 2001.

Newman, Susan. *It Won't Happen to Me: True Stories of Teen Alcohol and Drug Abuse*. New York: Perigree, 1987.

Roleff, Tamara L., and Helen Cothran, eds. *Drug Abuse: Opposing Viewpoints*. San Diego: Greenhaven Press, 2004.

Ryan, Elizabeth A. *Straight Talk About Drugs and Alcohol*. New York: Checkmark Books, 1996.

Silverstein, Alvin, Virginia Silverstein, and Robert Silverstein. *The Addictions Handbook*. Berkeley Heights, NJ: Enslow Publishers, 1991.

Addiction Science Network

http://www.addictionscience.net/

Alcoholics Anonymous

http://www.alcoholics-anonymous.org/

American Academy of Addiction Psychiatry

http://www.aaap.org/

The National Center on Addiction and Substance Abuse at Columbia University

http://www.casacolumbia.org

The National Council on Alcoholism and Drug Dependence

http://www.ncadd.org/

National Institute on Drug Abuse

http://www.nida.nih.gov/

U.S. Department of Health and Human Services

http://www.health.org/

INDEX

PICTURE CREDITS

Adderall is a registered trademark of Shire Richwood Inc.; Antabuse is a registered trademark of Alpharma ApS; Ativan is a registered trademark of Wyeth Ayerst Laboratories; Campral is a registered trademark of Merck Santé s.a.s. Subsidiary of Merck KgaA; Coca-Cola is a registered trademark of the Coca-Cola Company; Dexedrine is a registered trademark of SmithKline Beecham; Dolophine is a registered trademark of Roxane Laboratories, Inc.; Narcan is a registered trademark of Endo Pharmaceuticals Inc.; Oxycontin is a registered trademark of Purdue Pharma LP; Revia is a registered trademark of DuPont Pharmaceuticals Co.; Ritalin is a registered trademark of Novartis Pharmaceuticals; Sudafed is a registered trademark of Pfizer; Valium is a registered trademark of Roche Products; Xanax is a registered trademark of Pfizer, Inc.; Zyban is a registered trademark of GlaxoSmithKline.

AUTHOR

Vatsal G. Thakkar, M.D., is an assistant professor of psychiatry at Vanderbilt University School of Medicine. He was raised in Tennessee by parents of Indian origin. Thakkar received his bachelor's degree from the University of Tennessee in Knoxville and his doctor of medicine from the University of Tennessee in Memphis. He currently is the medical director for the Vanderbilt Mental Health Center where he spends his time supervising residents in outpatient practice and directing a course for second-year medical students. Thakkar also maintains pursuits outside of psychiatry, including photography and filmmaking. His most recent photo exhibit, entitled Fortitude, consists of portraits of cancer survivors and hangs at the Vanderbilt-Ingram Cancer Center. He has also written and directed a short film, *Ravaged*, about the plight of a man with post-traumatic stress disorder, which debuted in 2001 and screened as recently as 2005.